M000019020

Rich? Or Poor?

My Family's Memoir

1900-49

Nerina Mosley Culler

Table of Contents

- *Jacob Moseley standing to the right of Lena Sykes. Her brother, Herbert Sykes on his horse.*

1900-1925

My Daddy, Jacob Mosley, was born January 23, 1900, to Robert and Maggie Key Mosley. Jacob was a direct descendent of West Mosley from Scotland. The Mosleys were hard working, God-honoring, landowners. Their farm was in Surry County, near Mount Airy, North Carolina.

They grew fields of corn, fields of hay, a field of fruit trees - mostly apple - and three to four large gardens each year. They raised dozens of chickens for meat and eggs, two cows for milk and butter and two work horses for all the required field work to raise ten acres of tobacco! Raising tobacco was a 12 - month - a - year, labor-intensive, dirty, at times boring, other times an extremely fast-paced job. And during the harvest months of July to October many, many days required twelve to fourteen hours in order to complete the day's work.

Jacob, being the oldest living son in his family, had to take on responsibilities beyond his physical capabilities. At the age of six, he split all the wood for the cookstove needed to cook two large meals each day. This job was his and his alone. If he didn't split the wood, then the breakfast and dinner (lunch) could not be cooked. This was a seven day a week job. At the age of 8, Jacob helped "prime" the tobacco leaves from their stalks. At the barn, Jacob, age 10, climbed the tier poles in the tobacco barn, reached down for the heavy sticks of green tobacco leaves, then lifted them to the poles. A very labor-intensive job for one so young! At the age of 12, he was given all the field work that required the horses, plowing, cultivating, and harvesting all the gardens, corn fields, and all ten acres of tobacco.

Jacob wasn't the only one working beyond his limit. His siblings were also, in the house, in the gardens, in the fields of tobacco, corn and hay, and always caring for the latest addition to the family.

Jacob's mother, Maggie, accompanied her children to the fields, leading in the work, in order to get the day's work accomplished. And many, many of those days, Jacob would look up and see his mother leaning over, vomiting from yet another pregnancy, but then slowly, after sitting for a few minutes, pale-faced and weary, resumed her work and stayed with it to the end of the day. (Maggie gave birth to 13 children which included a set of twins).

There was one job the tobacco plants required two to three times each summer as they matured: "worming".

This was a job the four oldest children worked without their mother's presence. Unsupervised, the two boys, Jacob and Claude, loved to tease their sisters, Effie and Bertie.

- *Jacob's father, Robert, his wife Maggie with their first five children.*

Tobacco worms selected the biggest, prettiest leaves on a plant to EAT. They could eat the leaf in only a day or two. The kids would each take a row of tobacco, and while walking down the row, searching for the worms, finding them easily where leaves were being eaten, pluck the worm from the underbelly of the leaf, fling it to the ground, busting it wide open, splattering its green guts on the ground surrounding it.

Jacob and Claude, being boys, teased their sisters as they moved down the row. When they caught the thumb-sized, fuzzy, grotesque green worms, they would act as if they were throwing the worms at them, instead of the ground. The girls would yell and scream, even dodge the pretend throws, for they hated just to look at the worms, much less have one busted against them, its green guts splattered all over their clothes!

The girls threatened to go to the house, leaving them to do all the "worming" alone. Next, they threatened to tell their daddy on them. If that didn't stop them, then telling their mother of their silly shenanigans would do the trick.

Finally, the boys, tired of teasing their sisters, "got down" to the business at hand. Jacob, being the fastest at the job, would often double back and help his sisters with their row, so they could continue down the field together, no one left behind.

Of all the tobacco related work, there were two chores that Jacob really despised. One, the "housing" of the heavy tobacco sticks in the barn, and the other was his work pants. He wore his one pair from spring to late October, when all the tobacco leaves were harvested. His one pair of work pants were never washed! That's right - NEVER washed for the entire season! This didn't concern Jacob until HOT July and even hotter August set in. With the workload increased, and the tobacco "gum" from the leaves covering his hands, arms, and pants in its sticky, smut black gum, making his pants stiff, so stiff that when he took them off at night, the pants would actually stand up straight on the floor. Boy, and talk about uncomfortable to put on the next morning, words can't fully describe. The stink, the stiffness, the black "gum" was disgusting, but Maggie simply had more work than she could possibly do. So, the one thing she didn't do was wash everyone's field clothes on a scrub board each week. To do so would require a full day's labor, and that was a day she didn't have from all her other necessary jobs.

Maggie encouraged the children to go to the creek behind and below their home and use the lye soap she kept made. They could wash their pants while still wearing them. The kids loved the break and would visit the creek several times a week in the late evening before dark, to scrub not only their clothes, but themselves as well. This bath did seem to help remove some of the black "goo" off their pants, and soften them somewhat, but the next day, the tobacco "gum" clung even more than ever to their clothes. Their clothes were so stinky that when they entered the yard from their day in the field, the cats and kittens ran rapidly to the barn with old hound dog loping along behind them, to the cow stalls where it did not stink so bad!

In the meantime, the family had to contend with seasons when days, sometimes, even weeks, without sufficient rain, causing stunted growth of the plants, to seasons of too much rain, which, in lower fields caused the tobacco plants to "drown-out", turning them yellow, and unproductive. Also, windstorms and one summer, a severe hailstorm reduced the leaves to mere pieces lying on the ground, to fighting insects, worms, and plant diseases, to the everyday chores of milking two cows, feeding the chickens and horses, keeping wood for the cookstove available, the weekly laundry and house cleaning. There were physical work-related injuries, and one season the entire family suffered with a contagious influenza, putting everyone to bed for days.

Working with the horses was Jacob's favorite farming activity. The horses were mild tempered and always cooperative. They walked side-by-side pulling their load equally and turned smoothly whenever Jacob merely pulled their reins and called out "gee" or "haw" as to the direction to turn. Plus, working with the horses freed him from the boring jobs of chopping weeds from the tobacco, corn, and gardens, and the responsibility of splitting the stove wood every day. In addition, working and caring for the horses was considered "man's work", and earned Jacob a highly respected position with his family and people in the neighborhood. Plus, the best benefit, was Jacob had more time for school.

Jacob attended school at White Plains Elementary. Many days, to get a start on the day's work, he rose before daylight, ate his breakfast, then he worked until nearly time for school. Then, he ran the three miles to get to school on time for his first class. After school, he hurried home, back to the field and would work until dark. He kept all the field work requiring the horses fulfilled, and ready in advance.

White Plains school was open 5 months a year, and the 3 R's: reading, 'riting, and 'rithmatic were the classes taught. In addition, he had the ability to correctly spell all words, even words he had never heard before, by breaking the word into syllables, and then spelling each syllable correctly. Jacob graduated the tenth grade with honors, and this qualified him to teach school in Surry County, North Carolina and Patrick County, Virginia.

Due to a shortage of teachers, and Jacob's desire to try a new endeavor, Jacob accepted, at the age of 17, his first teaching job. Jacob enjoyed working with the kids, and the small check he received each month. He used the money to make a one-time yearly payment on a new 1918 model T Ford. He was the youngest man in Surry County to own and drive such a majestic roadster. But gradually, a little more each season, he became bored with spending his days in a room full of children. The majority of the youngsters were willing, even eager to study and learn. Their parents were appreciative of his time and effort in helping their children achieve an education, and therefore a more prosperous future than raising tobacco would provide for them.

Jacob missed working outside, under blue skies, tired of the strict school hours and regulations. So, after four seasons teaching, he decided to take a break, and returned home. Maybe something else, a job, or an opportunity, might present itself and he would be more satisfied with his efforts to earn a living.

After Jacob left teaching, he moved back home, to live in his mother's old homeplace, behind and below the Mosley home. Her father, David Key, had on his deathbed, given the house and land to her, for he knew she loved the place and would keep the taxes paid on it, and hand it on to one of his grandchildren. So, when Jacob asked her for permission to live there, she instantly agreed, on one condition: he improve the soil, enabling it to be productive again, and make needed repairs on the house. In return, he could grow tobacco or any other crop he pleased. She did not want a share of the crops he grew, which being the owner of the land, she had the perfect right to request.

Jacob raised pigs to sell, chickens for their eggs, even fields of corn to be ground into feed for cows - but to no success - for nobody - NOBODY - in his neighborhood had the money to buy his products or they raised their own.

So for the next four years, Jacob bartered with neighbors and traded his pigs for a milk cow, two work horses, a wagon, and several pieces of farm equipment. In addition to raising pigs, he kept his promise to his mother. He cleared the fields of overgrowth shrubs, rebuilt the fences, spread manure over the land, resulting in the lush green fields.

Yes, bartering had been good to him, but it would not buy gas or tires for his car, his cigarettes, or buy what groceries: coffee, flour, sugar, salt, pepper, etc. for his table. So, he began raising tobacco again, in hopes of providing the essentials that must be purchased. Jacob was content. He enjoyed being outdoors doing his own thing. He was proud of his improvements on the land and house. Even more important, his mother's appreciation of his work on her old homeplace.

But his nights were lonely. Please, Dear Heavenly Father, I need someone to love and who would love me in return, he often asked.

Then, he met Lena.

Lena was a shy, attractive girl raised by loving parents. She had not been able to attend school during her early years because of the three mile walk to school through the woods. Lena had three older brothers who walked the route to school, but then only on days they weren't needed at home to help with the 12-month-a- year job of raising tobacco. Lena did not work in the tobacco fields, but she and her mother, Sally, did work in the huge garden from mid-March to late September raising a full variety of vegetables to feed the family. With three growing, robust, highly spirited boys, it was quite an undertaking and challenge to keep their appetites satisfied.

The family kept two milk cows, two horses, and each year they raised three pigs and dozens of chickens. The boys and their father, James, hunted the fields and woods surrounding their share-croppers farm, often bringing home squirrels, rabbits and deer. They even occasionally brought in frog legs, fish, and turtles from the nearby creek.

Lena and her mother spent most of their days growing, preserving, drying and smoking the family's food supply. It was work they both enjoyed doing and was fully appreciated by the four male family members. One of the family's favorite winter meals was: dried green beans (leather britches), fresh deer meat stew, and small dried apple pies, fried to perfection. Oh boy, how delicious!

During the winter months, Lena and her mother sat near the fireplace, repairing and patching the men's work clothes. They also made quilts from discarded winter clothes and coats. The old clothes were cut into wide strips and the strips were sown together until they were bed size. Next, two layers were "tacked" together. Each bed held four of these quilts. Four quilts were so heavy, the sleeper found changing positions during the night somewhat clumsy.

In addition to the quilts, Lena and Sally placed a fresh supply of chicken feathers into the mattress pads covering each bed. These pads were warmed by the fireplace, and then laid on the bed's mattress, providing underneath warmth for the sleeper. The four heavy quilts, plus the heated pads, provided a toasty, cozy night's sleep, in the unheated, uninsulated bedrooms on bitterly cold nights, to everyone's total contentment.

Lena had five dresses: one summer church dress, one winter church dress, two for inside house work, and the final one specifically for garden and yard work. It was a very old dress and okay if it received further stains. All of Lena's dresses were made by the same pattern: long sleeves to the wrist, all the way up to the neck, with a collar, and a long flowing skirt down to her ankles. Whenever Lena went outside the door, whether to work, walk, or play, she wore gloves, stockings, and a large homemade bonnet with a six-inch brim around the sides to shade her face, and a wide ruffle across the bottom to shade her neck. No true, southern lady dared to let her skin get tan, as a two-toned skin was a sign of working in fields and therefore signified poverty. Sure, the family was poor, just managing to survive, but that did not prevent them from being proud, honest and a grateful God-honoring family.

Jacob, during his early 20's had spoken to several girls at church and social gatherings. He had visited three or four different girls in their homes, with their parent's permission, of course, but there had been no connection with anyone. Then one Sunday, he looked across the church to see new visitors entering the door. The four gentlemen, all tall and stately, sat on the left side of the church. The mother and her tall, attractive daughter sat on the right, as was customary in the Primitive Baptist Church.

When the service was over, Jacob looked back at the young lady, and thought, "Oh she's okay, nothing out of the ordinary." As he was thinking this, Lena stood up to leave the church. Instantly, Jacob's opinion of her changed. She stood tall with a straight back and graceful carriage. She had a glowing complexion with brilliant blue eyes and a shy, endearing smile. Jacob felt his heart give a tug as he walked towards her, hoping to speak to her before the family left the church.

Jacob walked over to James and introduced himself. James already had heard of Jacob Mosley, an outstanding young man from a highly respected family in the area. After a polite, short conversation, Jacob asked James if he could visit his daughter at her home later that afternoon.

James thought for a few minutes about their age difference, Jacob, being 25, and Lena, only 17. Their education difference, Jacob, a schoolteacher, Lena having taught herself to read and write. Their financial differences, Lena's family poor, share-crop farmers, and the Mosley's successful farmers and landowners.

Then, James looked at Jacob and saw the look of admiration on his face as he looked at Lena.

"Yes," James said, "You may visit her this afternoon."

James thought to himself, "We'll see if you're really interested in her."

At two o'clock, Jacob arrived at the Sykes home, still dressed in his church suit, just as dashing and good looking as this morning, Lena quietly noticed each time she glanced his way.

The living room contained a couch and two chairs across from it. Lena sat on one corner of the couch, Sally next to her, with James in the other corner. Jacob was offered one of the chairs. James conversed with Jacob until nearly dark. Jacob didn't get an opportunity to even speak to Lena, only glances and smiles were exchanged.

As Jacob exited the home, he asked if he could return next Sunday after church. He was cordially invited back.

During their eight-month courtship, the tension relaxed between Jacob and Lena's family. The two were allowed to converse together, to exchange ideas on church, his family, neighbors and their activities, the events taken place in the community, their likes and dislikes, and their hopes for the future as they became fully acquainted with each other. They sat in the living room, took walks over the farm, visited the horses, cows, pigs, and even walked to the creek to fish, but the best activity was the short rides in Jacob's car to visit friends and neighbors.

Both families attended the same church service every Sunday. There were several Primitive Baptist Churches in the surrounding area, and each church had a one Sunday a month service. So, when it wasn't the first Sunday (Old Hollow's Church Day), then members would attend another Primitive Baptist Church in the area.

James came to trust Jacob completely, for Jacob was a true southern gentleman. Nonetheless, Jacob and Lena were always accompanied by one of Lena's brothers the entire length of their courtship. Jacob did occasionally get a chance to hold Lena's hand, and even more rarely, a kiss on the cheek.

The attraction, the chemistry, the love between them spoke volumes for everyone to see. Lena knew she truly loved Jacob; his looks, his belief in our Heavenly Father, his ambitions, his wonderful sense of humor, EVERYTHING about him. She also knew there would never be another man for her. Jacob had totally captured her heart, and Jacob fully and completely reciprocated her love.

Finally, Jacob asked James for Lena's hand in marriage. James gave his consent and sincere blessings and the next meeting day at Old Hollow, two weeks away, was decided to be their wedding day.

James had anticipated this outcome and with the money he gave Lena, encouraged her to purchase white dressy fabric to make a wedding gown and veil. He also had money for matching dress shoes.

Lena had already decided instead of a long white gown that could only be worn occasionally, (even after she had shortened its length to a dress length). She preferred a nice dress she could wear to church, funeral services, family weddings, and other special events, giving her more service from the fabric. On her wedding day, Lena was glowing, but then she would have in any outfit. She was so in love and happy.

Church members, members of both families, numerous neighbors and friends, even several families where Jacob had taught their children, attended the wedding. The church was packed full.

Huge, old-growth trees surrounded the church with several of them in the yard behind the church. Between three of these trees, two-by-four short boards had been nailed nearly waist-high to each tree. Next, wide boards were nailed to the two-by-fours forming two tables 4 yards long between each tree. The boards were covered with tablecloths, making an appealing place to serve the appetizing dishes most of the guests and families had brought with them:

- Fried and baked chicken, roast pork, pots of beef stew, each with different seasonings, and several pots of deer and rabbit stews.
- There were large pots of vegetables, potatoes – fried and baked. Stewed green beans, sweet potato casseroles, black-eyed peas, green peas, turnip greens, wild creasy greens, beets, cucumber pickles, chopped onions, chow-chow, and relishes.
- Platters with both cornbread and biscuits were served on the ends of each table.
- Next were the pies: buttermilk, apple, pumpkin, cherry, small, dried apple pies,

even a couple of chocolate pies, which the children almost fought over, they wanted a slice so badly. Cakes, white and yellow, with frostings, and several puddings; peach, persimmon, wild blueberry, blackberry, even egg and bread puddings with nuts and raisins.

- And numerous containers of coffee, water, wild fox grape juice sweetened with honey, even lemonade, which again the children rushed to get a glass before it was gone.

    The day was mild and sunny, and everyone absolutely agreed it had been perfect. They praised God's Blessings on Jacob and Lena and their new life together.

Irish Blessing

May Love and Laughter Light Your Days
And Warm Your Heart and Home
May God and Faithful Friends Be Yours
Wherever You May Roam
May Peace and Plenty Bless Your World
With Joy That Long Endures
May All Life's Passing Seasons
Bring The Best to You and Yours.

When She Held Me In Her Arms

Through a market, I wandered and prayed
That I'd find me a woman I might marry someday.
Well, I never dreamed when I prayed that prayer
That the woman I longed for was standing there.

When she held me in her arms that night,
I held her close, and I held her tight.
And I swore that day forth, I'd love her all of my life.
When she held me in her arms that night.
She smelled of the sweetest lilac skin.
And I admit it now it drew me in
Oh, her voice cast a spell I could not disobey.
Every word was a river that swept me away.
Oh, the market became a more beautiful place:
The flowers more fragrant, and the clothing all lace.
And her eyes, oh, her eyes! They begged me to stay
And twenty years later, I've not regretted a day.

1925-1935

Lena enjoyed life. She even made "light" of her never-ending daily chores. "I'm playing," she'll say when anyone asks her what she was doing. When working in the garden, when weeding her flower beds, when serving the family, or the rare occasion when she had the ingredients to make chocolate or brown sugar pies for her family, when she washed clothes and laid them out on bushes to dry and the day was clear, warm, with a light breeze, ensuring the clothes a rapid dry and a luscious small. When canning fruits and vegetables for the coming winter's table, and even when cleaning the windows or scrubbing the floors, she made "light" of it.

Everything Lena did, she worked with willingness, a joy of life, and a positive attitude. Hard work was a way of life and being productive was a joy to her, but real play was dealt with in all seriousness. On cold winter evenings,

when the day's work was done, Lena and Jacob often
played a game of Rook. Lena took the game seriously, she

- *Lena with her brother Herbert Sykes.*

was determined that Jacob would not win the game, and she won more times than she lost.

Lena fully believed we needed something we truly enjoyed doing just for the pleasure of it and the joy it gave us. So, most nights sitting by the fireplace, with light from the kerosene lamps, she read and studied books, newspapers, anything the families and neighbors had passed on. She was not content with her limited education, so she continued her home study. Lena had an excellent memory and retained nearly everything she learned.

- Lena drank six to eight tall glasses of water each and every day. She believed, not drinking enough water could cause the blood to thicken, overworking the heart, and this could lead to fatigue, even fainting. Also, a glass of water before meals, fills the stomach the same as food, resulting in eating less.
- Lena had two church dresses. They were made from quality fabrics, fit her perfectly, and the colors enhanced her complexion. Two dresses were far better than none, and she was grateful for them.
- She never had any money to buy items she could use, but she already had everything she TRULY needed. All she had to do was to take care of them. One of these items was her dresses. She protected them (even the stained "outdoor" work dress) from further stains and tears, by covering them with an apron. The aprons were made from the backs of old dresses, and from empty feed sacks. All her aprons completely covered the front and sides, nearly to the hem of her dress with a large bib over the chest of each dress. Each contained two double stitches pockets, to hold items as she went about her daily chores. The aprons were worn ALL day, EVERY day, except when she attended church. The aprons

truly helped save her dresses giving them a much longer and productive life.

- She did not repeat gossip. She seldom heard derogatory remarks about another person but when she did, it went NO farther.
- She never compared herself to another woman, doing so could lead to feelings of inferiority. That was the same as telling her Heavenly Father: "You didn't make me as pretty as you made her!"
- She did not envy women who could drive a car or were in training to be a nurse or schoolteacher. She simply asked Jesus to "Bless each one in her endeavor".
- She knew two women who had suffered unbearably with crippling polo. They would require both braces and crutches for the rest of their lives in order to slowly walk from room to room of her home. Lena realized, "But for the Grace of God, I go."
- She lived one mile from a family with five small children and a very neglectful alcoholic husband/father. Lena managed to share something with the mother every week, even though it was only a small bag of potatoes, or apples, or a gallon bucket of cooked pinto beans, or just a gallon of milk. Lena knew her gifts were small, but if other families in the neighborhood would do the same, maybe then the children would not be so hungry.
- She was grateful for living in a home that did not leak when it rained and could be kept comfortably warm even on the coldest January nights. The home had a bountiful spring for water about 15 yards from the kitchen door. How convenient!
- She and Jacob had NO money to buy anything, (as was very common with all the families in the area), but their family always had plenty to eat, and had yet to go to bed hungry!

- She was BOTH happy and proud to be Jacob's wife. They had so much in common and their love and admiration for each other continued to grow. Lena's only concern was Jacob's severe bouts of melancholy(depression). Oh, how sad, to see him so quiet, withdrawn, and full of self-loathing, because he was not able to provide better for his family.
- She deeply loved her three young daughters the Heavenly Father had blessed her and Jacob with during the ten years of their marriage. She was amazed at the miracle of their birth, and their excellent health, and beauty.
- Lena's TRUE happiness was centered in Jesus Christ, her Lord & Savior. With Jesus living in her heart/soul she was enveloped in Peace and Contentment. Plus, she treasured and held near His Promise that she would spend ALL Eternity in His Presence, in Heaven, with Him and the Heavenly Father. What Blessed Assurance! Thank you, Father, Son, and Holy Spirit, for Peace with you is EVERYTHING!

IRELAND

Lena's ancestors were from Ireland and though she was never able to visit Ireland, she loved the country, the character of the people, the history, the traditions, and the customs. She could picture, in her mind, the gently rolling green fields, hear the rush of the ocean against the shore, the Bonnie Blue skies with huge fluffy white clouds, feel the sea breeze against her cheeks, the sound of the seagulls calling, the chill of winter nights and the warmth of the summer days.

"You can leave Ireland," she'll say, "but Ireland will never leave you. Ireland is as much a part of me as breathing."

- *a Sykes family gathering*

Lena kept a book of Irish blessings and old Irish/Scottish songs. "Oh, how I enjoy reading the blessings and I especially love when Jacob sings those old ballads." Three or four evenings a week after supper, during warm weather, sitting on the front porch, they sang the songs as the sun slowly set and darkness filled the yard.

She sang the songs as entertainment, as encouragement, as a past time, as a hobby, in times of joy and happiness, and in times of worry and anxiety. The songs brightened her spirit, lightened her load, and sustained her.

Lena loved to hear bagpipes playing. Several Christmases, Jacob took Lena to the Christmas parade in Mount Airy, just to see the marching bagpipes band.

"Just look at the bands brightly colored kilts, their ghillies, their tan berets. Just look at their precision marching! Just listen to the beautiful music the bagpipes are playing! It gives me chills from the top of my head to the bottom of my toes!"

Jacob didn't know which he enjoyed the most, the band and their music, or Lena's radiant face and enthusiasm as the band marched by.

- *Jacob and Lena with a neighbor and his cow in front of a field of tobacco.*

1935

The "dirty thirties" had been financially severe on American families all over the United States. The stock market crash, the loss of public jobs, the bank closures, the factory shutdowns, the dead economy, had resulted in the great depression. No jobs, no money, no credit, most victims were living in extreme poverty, on the verge of starvation and even homelessness.

- *The new homeplace in the southwest tip corner of Patrick County. Virginia*

Jacob was blessed to be living on his mother's old homeplace where he grew tobacco to earn a yearly income. He worked 6 days a week most weeks. Even on days rain had left the ground too wet to work, many other things that needed to be accomplished to raise and harvest seven acres of tobacco each year. He worked eight hours every day, up to fourteen hours per day during harvest time. But, there were several labor-intensive, time-consuming, requirements to raising a crop of tobacco that NO ONE could possibly accomplish on his own. So, each grower would "swap" work with another grower, (a neighbor, relative, friend, etc. and his family) to get the crops raised and harvested. This "swapping" started with the "sitting out" of the small plants from the plant beds to the fields of countless fertilized ridged rows each May.

- *The new homeplace with the driveway in the first picture. Second picture shows some of Lena's flowers down the driveway.*

- The constant battle with weeds until the tobacco seedlings grew large enough to "crowd out the intruder, which occurred around July 4th each year. Now, the farmer could enjoy a two-week break from his tobacco fields. The fields had been "laid by"

- Next, came the "priming" of three to six ripening leaves starting at the ground. Then, again, in six to seven days, moving up the stalk and "priming" (by hand-1 leaf at a time) another 3-6 leaves. It usually required 7-8 weeks to completely remove all the leaves as they ripened.
- As the men primed the green leaves, they laid them by the arm-full into an eight foot long "sled". The sled was pulled down the tobacco rows by each farm's work horse or mule. Mules were used more often than horses, because they could endure the sun's hot rays better than a horse and could work the fields for a longer period of time. There needed to be no less than 4, (6 would be better) men priming in order to get the job done efficiently and timely. The mule or horse pulled the full load of leaves to the barn to be "tied".
- The "tying" was women's work. The "tyer" needed to be very fast in wrapping a string around the small handful of leaves onto the one-inch-square oak tobacco stick. This operation required at least a total of 5 people to get the sled empty before the next one arrived.
- When the "primers" came in for lunch or again at the end of the day, everyone "pitched-in" to "house" the sticks of tobacco into the barn.
- Two or three men climbed up into the barn and stood, right foot on the "tier pole" right of him and his left foot on his left. He would reach down for the heavy stick of green leaves, lift it to his chest, then over his head to the "houser" standing on the

27

pole above him. This work continued until the barn was filled.

- One laborious, even frustrating job EVERYONE had to do EVERY DAY was to wash the BLACK "tobacco gum" from their hands before they could eat lunch or supper. The gum was so thick and sticky, it required scrubbing with soap, an old cloth, and water to remove!

- The job of "topping could be done by one person, if need be. A "hard-worker" could walk down the row and break off the very top 6-8 inches of the stalk when flowers were blossoming into glorious lavender blooms. If the blooms were allowed to mature and make seeds, this would weaken the plant, making it susceptible to plant diseases.

- "Suckering" was another job the farmer could work alone. Walking down the row, he would remove the small new leaves coming out of the stalk where another leaf had already flourished big and healthy. If this sucker leaf was allowed to grow, it would cause the large leaf to fall from the stalk and cold weather would prevent the sucker leaf from making a large leaf that the farmer could sell.

- Late November, early December was "clean-up" time on the farms. Harvesting the corn (one ear at a time), plowing the corn fields and gardens plus getting the tobacco fields ready for the coming year's planting. The fields of naked tobacco stalks were plowed from the ground. Everyone chose a row, picked up the stalks and placed them in piles every 25-30 feet apart. Each evening (when the winds were calm) the piles were set on fire. The fires were kept burning until the debris had been totally consumed. This usually required most of the night. This burning helped to prevent plant diseases from spreading from one crop year to the next.

Once the barn was filled with green tobacco leaves, a very small fire was built and each flue and kept alive for 24-36 hours, allowing the leaves sufficient time to turn yellow-hopefully a "Bright" shade of yellow.

Next, the fires were increased gradually and kept burning BOTH day and night until the inside of the barn was a maintained 85° F, and the stems of the leaves gradually lost all their moisture (no buyer would buy leaves if he found just one swollen stem in the bunch, as one indicated more could be present-and this could cause the whole bunch to become molded with mildew-a HUGE NO! NO!

- *Lena and Jacob with their three daughters, Iona standing, Audrey sitting on her father's lap and Mable on her mother's knee.*

When the barn full of leaves had finished "curing", they were dry and brittle, so the barn door was left open all night to allow the night's moisture to enter the leaves. Sometimes, dry weather made it necessary to keep the door open for 2 nights and occasionally to even lay a fine mist of water on the dirt floor of the barn.

Very early next morning, while the dew was still on the ground, the family moved the sticks of tobacco via wagon and carried them to the "pack house" where they were laid in a neat pile. This packed the leaves, enabling them to lay flat & smooth.

Next, when the farmer wasn't "priming" or busy in other field work, the family moved the cured tobacco through a 4x6 foot hole in the pack house floor, to the plain dirt basement below so the sticks of cured tobacco could receive even more moisture.

The sticks of tobacco were hung on the basement's tier poles to receive more moisture. One -two days later, the sticks were taken down, the leaves stripped from the stick and laid on the small earth floor near the outside door of the basement. There the leaves were sorted into 3 different grades: 1) (and hopefully the largest amount) was the big "Bright Leaf", the buyers sought. The 2) still, nice leaves, just not quite "up to par" as the Bright Leaf. The third bundle was the "scrap leaves", dark with green and brown stripes that were seldom purchased.

Next, a handful of the stems were gathered and held tightly in the farmer's left hand as he crunched the stems tightly together. A nice colored leaf was chosen, then folded in half-length wise over the farmer's knee, and using both hands, the farmer wrapped the folded leaves around the stems 3 or 4 times to ensure the "bundle" of leaves stayed together. The bundles were placed, stems outward onto a circle flat board. Finally, the farmer had tobacco ready to carry to the warehouse in Mount Airy to sell. He truly hoped and believed he would be paid top dollar for his tobacco.

For help with these projects, Jacob "swapped" labor with the Joe Johnson Family, who lived 1 mile beyond Jacob's house. The Johnson Family had 3 young children and continued to welcome an additional infant every 2 years! For Joe and Nancy (his wife) to help in the Jacob's crop, Lena cared for Nancy's two youngest children from early spring straight through to the final sale of their tobacco in the fall. This made a nearly full-time job for Lena, but by doing this, Lena could stay with her own young daughters and not have to take them to the fields and barns. Plus, this arrangement also helped Jacob with his labor needs, so both families benefited from this arrangement.

Lena MADE time to work in the huge garden each year, even if it was only 1 to 3 hours at a time. Most days Lena worked shortly after breakfast, before the sun became too hot for her daughters and Nancy's two youngest children and herself. And some days after the sun had cooled, she would some days go back to the garden and work until dark.

Starting with the first daughter, Lena placed the small girl(s) into their playpen under the huge oak tree located to the left of the garden. The girls were fascinated as they watched the new spring kittens playing near them and especially when one or two of the kittens entered the playpen searching for food and then to lay down and fall asleep on the quilt covering the playpen's floor. Even the hound dog laid by the playpen to "guard" the girl(s) --- that is when he wasn't sleeping. Lena kept water bottles, biscuits, and clean diapers, with the girls, which provided more time for her to work in the garden. Lena worked swiftly and efficiently, the few hours she had available. Each year, she had managed to feed the family. After all, they couldn't eat tobacco!

The fields of tobacco had earned a small profit (after expenses) the first eight years of their marriage. However, the extreme dry weather of the past two years had ruined Jacob's tobacco crop. Dry weather left the plants unable to grow, with a few small, thin leaves the tobacco buyers would NOT purchase. Tobacco is a weed, and like ALL weeds, tobacco needed moisture to grow. By 1934 & 1935, Jacob did not earn enough money from his tobacco to pay for the fertilizer to grow it! Not to mention all the other expenses involved in raising a crop of tobacco!

- *Fire cured tobacco barn. The Moseley farm had four.*

The buyers walked the warehouse floor (three were located on side streets in Mount Airy). The buyers picked ONLY the "golden yellow" leaves and NONE of the bunches were bought where the buyer had found a soft, swollen stem. This left the farmers with large quantities of tobacco to be returned home. At home, the farmers, scattered the leaves over their fields, then plowed them into the ground, and hopefully this would enrichen the soil for next year's crop.

Jacob realized the tobacco farmers were caught between a rock and a hard place, beyond their control. No one could make a profit raising tobacco until or unless the government stepped in and "allotted" a small acreage to each farmer, limiting the amount of tobacco grown. Hopefully this limited supply would increase the price for the farmers.

Until this quota was enforced, Jacob vowed never to raise another crop of tobacco. Jacob couldn't help but hope the depression would lift and the economy would soon improve. Jacob asked the men at church, and in his neighborhood, and his dad, what they thought of the farming opportunities coming. Jacob also read the "Progressive Farmer," magazine, which was published fourteen times a year in Winston Salem, North Carolina, offering advice to farmers.

The magazine stated growing peaches in the foothills of the Blue Ridge Mountains would produce larger, juicier, more delicious peaches, than the small, tasteless peaches grown in the sandy soils of Georgia, North Carolina, and South Carolina. The poor selling of their peaches was causing many small orchardists in those states to go out of business, opening the market for Virginia peaches.

After giving the situation much thought, Jacob, fully believed raising peaches was the wave of the future for small farmers such as himself. He knew apples were successfully grown and sold from the foothills of Patrick County, why shouldn't Peaches do the same?

Jacob asked Mr. Sawcott, President of the First National Bank in Mount Airy, if he knew of any farm for sale that would be suitable for a peach orchard. Mr. Sawcott told Jacob of a sixty-acre farm located in the southwestern tip of Patrick County, Virginia, just across the state line from North Carolina. The asking price for the farm was five hundred and twenty-five dollars. A SMALL FORTUNE!

"Just go look at the place," Mr. Sawcott recommended to Jacob and Lena. "It needs a little work, but it is a great place. Go look at it, then come back tomorrow and tell me what you think of the place. If you like it, the bank will finance it for you."

Later, as Jacob and Lena stood in the back yard of the farm and looked out over the fields, they could plainly see that calling the place a "farm" was a serious misrepresentation. It was anything but a farm.

All the large timber had been cut from the land, leaving only huge stumps and scrub trees. The land was covered in blackberry patches, honeysuckle vines, and over-grown bushes.

There was clean land near the house for a garden and a pasture for their cow and two work horses. There was a barn in the back yard, with a sloping roof, but the roof had completely collapsed on one end. The barn contained two stalls for horses, a corn bin, and an area for storing farm equipment.

A hand-dug well, only twenty feet from the back door of the house, had been dug to the depth of forty-five feet but it was bone dry. The only water available for the needs of the family was a spring, located on the far side of the farm. The spring was nearly one hundred and fifty feet lower, plus three hundred yards from the house, which meant a long, sloping uphill walk back to the house with a full bucket, or buckets, of water. Two-peck buckets of water were heavy when picked up at the spring but seemed to weigh a ton long before the carrier ever reached the house, often setting the buckets down 2-3 times to rest.

The back yard was covered in trash, kitchen waste, and junk. There was a five-room house with a front and a back porch. At some point in time, the back door had blown open and stray dogs had been coming in and had made their home inside the house. The dogs had destroyed the old mattresses and other items the previous tenant had left behind. Every room was filled with trash and infested with lice, fleas, and bed bugs. The trash, the dog droppings, and the dead mice caused a stench so gross and foul that it was impossible to take a breath without retching.

The house, the yards, the barn, the fields--the entire place was the most neglected, most desolate place Lena had ever seen. Looking at the waste, Lena could only see years of hard work before the "farm" would ever be a productive place. Years of work, sacrifice, and frugal living and then maybe, just maybe, the place would be a farm and earn an income for the family.

But then, Jacob and Lena raised their eyes and looked to the north beyond the trash covered yard. There were the Blue Ridge Mountains. The mountains could be seen from the eastern sunrise, all the way to the evening sunset in the west, as far as the eye could see, in one solid ridge. The grandeur and beauty of those velvet blue mountains were breathtaking and awe-inspiring.

Jacob could feel God's presence while looking at those mountains. Jacob could sense His Majesty, His Power in creating such an amazing sight. God, the Great Jehovah, was here. Looking at the mountains, feeling God's presence, Jacob knew that with time, hard work, and the Almighty's Blessing, he could envision it in his optimistic mind's eye, a showplace of green fields and pastures, and a productive peach orchard with those vivid blue mountains as a backdrop!

Yes, Jacob thought, peaches was the crop that would make the farm prosperous and would produce the income necessary to ensure a secure future for the family.

The next morning, going against Lena's better judgment and plans to give the decision more time and thought, Jacob returned to the bank and together they borrowed the five hundred and twenty-five dollars to purchase the sixty-acre farm. Mr. Sawcott even allowed Jacob to borrow an extra $20 dollars to help with the expense of moving and to buy cleaning products and paint for every room of the house.

Before Lena would allow her three young daughters, Iona, nine, Audrey, six, and Mabel, two, to be moved, she needed to give each room a thorough cleaning. Lena sprayed each room and its trashy contents with a heavy spraying of DDT, then closed the doors to each room so the DDT could accomplish its job.

Jacob and Lena returned to the house three days later. She raised all the windows and opened all the doors to allow fresh air inside to rid the house of the horrible smell. With Jacob's help in moving the bigger, heavier items, Lena removed all the trash from each room. The debris was carried to the back yard and placed in a large pile for burning later. Lena then scrubbed all the floors with her homemade lye soap. The soap in a pail of water, along with Lena's determination, cleaned away the dirt and removed the horrible stench.

The following week, Lena and Jacob painted each room, in soft shades of beige. The turpentine in the paint finished killing any bed bugs remaining. The paint gave the entire house a fresh, clean smell. The house was finally ready for the family to move in.

Jacob owned a 1930 four-door Ford Sedan. It was used to move all the small household items to the new place. All the farm equipment and household furniture had to be hauled there by Jacob's horse-drawn wagon.

The first load of furniture, along with Sweet Pea, the cow, tied behind the wagon, took a full 8 hours to travel the fourteen miles to their new home. The workhorses, "Sadie" and "Neil," required frequent stops to rest from pulling the heavy load. These stops were especially needed on the sections of the road which were on an incline. Also, it would not be good for Sweet Pea to get overtired or distracted since she was needed to provide milk for the family's supper.

Three more trips were required to get everything to the new home. On Jacob's final load, he decided to stop at the country store closest to his new place as this would be the store he'd use for the few items the family would be needing in the weeks and months ahead.

As he entered the store, a black man stood behind the counter. Immediately he called, "Come in, come in," with a big smile, as he walked to Jacob and cordially shook his hand.

His name was Milton Ward and he fully believed that what you give out was exactly what you'd receive in return. Give out sincere warmth, friendship, and respect, and you'd receive these qualities back just as quickly; give out coldness, resentment, and disrespect, you'd receive that back as well. Milton fully and totally believed: "Do unto others as you would have them do unto you," and this he lived by every day.

Both men had a crazy sense of humor, each learned of the other as they talked and became more acquainted.

Jacob asked, "Do you know Fred Smith who lives just about a mile down the road?"

"I've heard the name," Milton replied.

"Well Fred and his wife loved airplanes, and truly wanted to ride in one, but couldn't afford the asking price. So, this fall, at the fair, a pilot brought his small plane and was giving rides for just three dollars. Fred handed the pilot the money, then he and his wife began to enter the plane.

"Wait a minute," the pilot said, "That's three dollars a person."

"But I don't have any more money and I'm not going to ride without her. She wants to ride just as badly as I do."

The pilot thought for a minute, then replied, "Okay, I'll take both of you for a ride, as long as you stay completely quiet and don't make a sound, I can't stand people screaming while I am in the air, so if you do, then the fee for the flight will double to twelve dollars for the two of you.

Smith agreed to the terms offered, so the pilot took them high in the sky, he did dives and rollovers, he even flew upside down. When they finally landed, the pilot said to the man, "you did good. I never heard a sound from you."

"I know," answered Smith, "but it really was hard to keep quiet when my wife fell out of the plane."

GARDEN

With hopeful enthusiasm, Jacob and Lena tackled the monumental job ahead of them. The priority was getting the garden cleaned and plowed, ready for early spring planting of vegetables. The garden was of utmost importance since it had to provide the food the family would depend on during the coming year. No garden, no food, it was just that simple and just that complicated.

To help fetch the badly needed water from the spring located on the backside of the farm, Jacob built a small sled that tightly held 4 water buckets. On the uphill return to the house, each trip was slow and tedious to prevent the water from splashing over the rim of the containers. But this sure beat Jacob having to carry the heavy buckets himself, plus it saved time too. This trip was made twice every day, even up to four times, many days, regardless of the weather.

In addition to fetching the water, each day's work consisted of cutting the scrub trees into the wood for the cook-stove and fireplace. Also, feeding the horses and milking Sweet Pea twice daily, and cooking two meals each day and this was only a part of each day's chores.

As Christmas drew closer and closer, Lena became more and more concerned about the disappointment her daughters would have at getting no gifts from Santa Claus on Christmas morning. Lena gently explained to the girls that the TRUE meaning of Christmas was not in the gifts Santa brought them, but was in the gift which God, our Heavenly Father, had given in the birth of His Son, our Lord, and Savior, Jesus Christ.

The girls had listened intently to their Mama's explanation of the real meaning of Christmas, but she still wanted the girls to wake up on Christmas morning to at least one small present each.

After dark each night, after the girls were asleep, by the light of the burning wood in the fireplace and a nearby kerosene lamp, Lena "set about" to make as good a Christmas as possible for the girls. Searching through the "rag bag" of old castoff clothing which no one could further use, Lena studied what she could make for the girls using those items.

"Waste not, want not," Lena said. "Everything has a use and a purpose, and with a little imagination in a time of need everything can be used in numerous ways."

From this "stash" Lena designed and then made three twelve-inch cloth dolls with arms and legs. Lena carefully embroidered eyes, nose, and a cute mouth on each of the faces. The dolls were stuffed with soft rags. Long hair was made with layer upon layer of pleated strips of fabric stitched into place.

Lena, then made dresses, bonnets, and blankets for each doll. The dolls were truly "works of art" and a labor of love.

Using narrow strips of wood Lena had rubbed until all surfaces were smooth, she made a bed for each doll. From the "rag bag", Lena cut apart two of her old dresses

40

and fashioned pillows, quilts, and a mattress for each small bed. Lena took three cardboard boxes, turning them on their sides to form a large bedroom. The rooms had three walls, a ceiling, and a floor inside each one. Using a cup of juice from the fox grapes Lena had canned back in the fall, and a piece of scrap cloth, she stained the inside and outside walls, floors, and ceiling of the crates, turning the boxes into bedrooms for the dolls. Using glue she made by mixing a little water with a small amount of flour, Lena "pasted" fabric onto the floors for rugs and added curtains for windows.

In addition to beds, Lena made three "dresser drawers" from empty matchboxes. She glued the boxes one on top of the other, four boxes high to form a chest of drawers. It was amazing how easily the drawers pulled out and back in, just like real drawers. Lastly, Lena used three-inch high round pieces of wood to form chairs. She covered the wood in fabric and sewed cushions to top each chair.

CHRISTMAS

When alone, Jacob and Lena silently talked to their Heavenly Father. They praised His Holy Name and honestly and sincerely thanked Him for His kindness, mercy, and love and for giving His beloved Son, Jesus Christ, to pay the penalty for mankind's sins.

They knew our Heavenly Father cannot and will not allow or accept sin to enter Heaven, making entering Heaven completely and totally impossible for sinners. Everyone who has ever lived is born with Adam's sin nature, alive and well, dwelling within them. But our Heavenly Father loves mankind and did not want them to perish and spend eternity in Hell for the punishment of their sins, instead, He wanted them to be able to spend ALL eternity in Heaven with Him. And the only way to accomplish this was to send His One and Only Begotten Son, Jesus Christ, to earth to pay our sin debt for us. Our sins were placed upon His sinless back to be punished and put to death in our place.

Then, by believing in Jesus, His Life, Death, Burial, and Resurrection and confessing our sins to our Father, sincerely repenting them, and asking for forgiveness, we are washed in Jesus's cleansing blood, our sins are forgiven. Then, with the indwelling power of the Holy Spirit, we are to live a God Honoring Life. In fact, Our Heavenly Father burrows our sins in the sea of forgetfulness to be remembered no more. We are free to come to Him in Love, Praise, and Supplication, and to lay our needs at His Feet. The family desperately needed food. As Christmas came closer, their small food supply dwindled smaller and smaller.

The dry spring and summer at their formal place had produced small yields of vegetables, despite the family's creaseless work to water the garden. Now, three days before Christmas, the family was down to just their home-made molasses and cornbread.

Since moving to this new place, every evening after supper and many mornings after tending to the cow and horses, Jacob, with his gun in tow, walked over the farm, and into the woods looking for squirrel, rabbits, and deer. He was able to get three rabbits on three different occasions, but never saw a deer. He reasoned the deer had been hunted to near extinction, due to men trying to provide food for their families during the depression.

Now, the days before Christmas Eve, the entire family was suffering with burning stomachs from the molasses and cornbread, and the thought of eating those again was more than even Jacob could tolerate.

Christmas Eve morning was cold, cloudy, and sad. Very sad and full of anxiety for both Lena and Jacob. How were they to feed their three small daughters, dear Lord?

Then, about ten o'clock, there was a knock at the kitchen door. Jacob opened the door to find a well-dressed man, about fifty, standing there. The man stepped inside the room and said to Jacob, "Mr. Mosely, I've come to pay you the money I owe you," and handed a bill to Jacob.

"No, you don't owe me any money," Jacob answered.

"Oh yes, I do." The stranger quickly answered, pushing the money closer to Jacob.

"No, I've never seen you before, so how can you possibly owe me any money?" Jacob responded.

"I'm sorry, you can't remember the time you helped me, and I promised that I would pay you as soon as I was able. So, here it is," as he grabbed Jacob's hand and put the bill in his hand, then, he turned and walked out the door.

Jacob stared at the money in his hand, unable to utter a word. A twenty-dollar bill. A TWENTY DOLLAR BILL! A small fortune! Lena rushed over and gushed as she stared at the money. Next, the three daughters gathered around, hardly able to believe their eyes, and started jumping up and down. Lena started crying and even Jacob shed tears. Their prayers had been answered.

Jacob looked out the kitchen door, on the back porch, across the yard, and then down the driveway. The gentleman was nowhere to be seen. Who was this man? Who could he have been?

Jacob knew that he could never carry home twenty dollars' worth of groceries, so he put on heavy clothing, then went to the barn and hooked the horses to the wagon. Milton Ward's store was about a 1/2 mile south. There Jacob purchased:

- A 25-pound bag of flour for $2.49
- Baking soda and baking powder for $0.30
- Fat-back meat, 10 pounds for $2.59
- One bushel of potatoes for $3.49

- 5-pound coffee for $1.25
- 10 pounds of white sugar for $0.56
- Pinto beans, 20-pound bag for $2.30
- 3 large boxes of matches for $0.50
- A large pouch of smoking tobacco and 5 packs of cigarette rolling paper for $1.85
- 3 dozen oranges for $1.40

And finally, the remaining $0.56 was used to purchase a box of stick horehound candy for the girls. All for a total of $20.00.

Jacob joyfully sang "Amazing Grace" in his clear rich baritone voice all the way home, and the still air carried the melody to the neighbors on his way. Several neighbors came to their door to raise a friendly hand to Jacob and cheerfully called out, "Merry Christmas," as he passed.

At home, Lena and the girls helped unload the wagon and bring the groceries to the kitchen. Lena quickly prepared a late lunch/ early supper for the family.

By dark the sky had cleared, the moon was shining brightly over the yard and land, even the beautiful blue mountain seemed to glow with joy. After dark, Lena prepared a warm place near the fireplace for the girls to lay down, while she and Jacob sat close to them. They sang songs of Grace, Mercy, and Love God bestowed upon His Children. On Christmas morning, the daughters were surprised and extremely thrilled with the beautiful dolls and the unique doll house with the "life-like" furniture. Santa Claus had truly come to their home during the night.
This was the Christmas the entire family always remembered and shared with everyone.

From the Primitive Baptist Songbook

How sweet the name of Jesus sounds,
In a believer's ear!
It soothes his sorrows, heals his wounds,
And drives away his fear.
It makes the wounded spirit whole,
And calms the troubled breast;
'Tis manna to the hungry soul,
And to the weary rest.
Dear name! The rock on which I build,
My shield and hiding place;
My never-failing treasury, filled
With boundless stores of grace.
Satan accuses me in vain,
And I am owned a child,
Jesus! My Shepherd, Husband, Friend,
My Prophet, Priest, and King,
My Lord, my Life, my Way, my End,
Accept the praise I bring.
Weak is the effort of my heart,
And cold my warmest thought;
But when I see thee as thou art,
I'll praise thee as I ought.
Till then I would thy love proclaim,
With ev'ry fleeting breath;
And may the music of thy name
Refresh my soul in death.

1936

Jacob was totally enthralled with the future the farm presented, and anxious to swiftly bring it to fruition - but also extremely concerned with how he was to finance the project during the coming four to five years (the time he allotted himself to accomplish this humongous endeavor) with NO income to purchase ALL the necessities this would require:

- Truckloads of fertilizer and limestone for the entire farm.
- Grass seed by the 25-pound bags to sow the hayfields, pastures, and orchard.
- Rolls of barbed wire to enclose the farm animals inside their pastures.
- Hundreds of peach tree seedlings necessary to plant the 22-acre orchard.
- Dynamite by the boxes to blast the largest stumps from the fields.
- A horse-drawn sprayer.
- The insecticides to control insects and fungicides to prevent leaf disease.
- A huge load of pre-cut wooden slabs to construct bushel baskets.
- In addition, the yearly payments of personal property taxes to be paid to Patrick County.
- The once-a-year large land payment which included the interest on the loan.
- Plus, the personal needs of the family; groceries, shoes, Jacob's cigarettes (he loved Camels), etc.
- A tin wood burning heater for the main bedroom.
- Another Jersey cow in order to always have a constant supply of milk, butter, and buttermilk.
- A small chicken house with enclosed fence to ensure the chickens' safety.

- A flock of baby chickens each spring.
- The gas and upkeep of the car.
- Kerosine for the household lamps and frequently used lanterns.
- In addition to the extreme cost of digging the well deeper in order to have water available and convenient for the family's needs.

How? How? This was the constant turmoil doing rapid circles inside Jacob's head, as he and Lena cleaned the yard and worked the one- third acre plot of land next to the house, preparing it for the coming seasons' gardens.

Finally, one night after supper, he asked, "Lena, what do you think of getting a job at the Mount Airy Knitting Mill to help get our peach orchard up and running? The worst of the depression is over, and they are hiring new employees to help fill the orders coming in."

- *Standing in the backyard looking north toward the Blue Ridge Mountains after Jacob had cleared the land.*

Lena didn't (couldn't) answer right away. The very thought of being surrounded by total strangers in a huge room with the constant roar of the sewing machines, filled her with extreme apprehension and self-doubt. Could she do the work as swiftly and as professionally as the mill required? Could she accomplish this five days a week -- in addition to all the necessary cooking, gardening, canning, tending to the cow, laundry? What about her three young daughters? Who would be there for them if she was gone ten hours a day?

But, on the other side, Lena knew Jacob would need to borrow more and more money to accomplish his goal, and by that time, they would be so deeply in debt, they could never pay it all back. They could even lose this beautiful home and have NO place to live!

"I won't worry about that possibility now." Lena thought, "Instead, just what's necessary for today. And that's that the well needs to be dug deeper. We absolutely MUST have water to live! And groceries. We have plenty of milk, butter, and buttermilk, but we need groceries, too."

"I don't know anything about working in a mill, but let's try and see if they'll give me a job," Lena told Jacob two days later.

Jacob drove Lena to the mill's office every morning for the next four mornings. On the fourth try, she was offered a job on the cutting floor. Lena accepted.

The cutting floor housed two long tables. Each table had an electric scissors/knife hanging from overhead, and could be moved from one end of the table to the other end. Also, over the tables, were huge rollers that spread the fabric, back and forth, back and forth, until it was eight dozen layers deep. A pattern was stamped on the top layer of fabric as a guide for the cutter.

That was Lena's job and responsibility: to cut the fabric on the exact pattern line, completely accurate. "A wrong cut could destroy the sown garments outcome", Betty Young, Lena's instructor/inspector warned her. "Start slow, learn and gradually pick-up speed as you go."

The first two days, Betty allowed Lena to work with scrap fabric to learn how to correctly handle the cutting knife, and as she learned to cut, Lena's speed in cutting gradually increased. At the end of Lena's second week, Betty told her, "You're doing great! Just continue to gradually pick-up speed, as you perfect your cutting. Quality and quantity both matters."

With sheer determination, and total concentration, not speaking to anyone, seldom taking a restroom break or getting a drink of water, Lena had the job conquered by the sixth weeks' time limit the mill allowed. Lena could perfectly cut hundreds of dozens of garments, then tie each eight-dozen bundle together with scrap fabric and place each bundle in a nearby metal roller bin to be moved to the sewing floor.

"You're a great worker, Lena," Betty told her, "You have a job with us for as long as you want it."

Lena earned 10 cents an hour and was paid every other Friday, (total time: 80 hours). The first check was richly rewarding and exciting for Lena. That was the MOST money she had ever held in her hand before, much less earned ALL on her own. She was proud of her accomplishment! Jacob was too!

ANDREW

The hand-dug well was bone dry when the family had moved to their new home, and with Lena working and gone from home ten hours per day, in addition to all the regular work required at home, the well had to definitely be dug deeper.

Jacob inquired of Milton if there was a "well-digger" anywhere in the surrounding area. Milton quickly answered, "Andrew Taylor, and I highly recommend him."

Andrew was a well-digger by trade. As with most black men in the area, he had to develop his own occupation and earn a living independently without a public job. There were only a few jobs available for white men, and nearly none for the black man. Andrew, and many other black men in the area, had developed an entrepreneurial spirit and had created their own business.

Andrew was a mild-mannered man who never got in a hurry. He could converse with anyone for hours at a time, as long as the other person was willing to communicate.

Andrew drove a 1910 hand cranked truck. The bed of the truck was loaded with the equipment needed to dig a well by hand: short-handled shovels, pick ax, buckets, wedges, ropes, boots, safety hats, gloves, and a small wooden box secured to the bed of the truck to hold sticks of dynamite.

Andrew charged fifty cents an hour, plus the cost of the dynamite used on the job. This was a huge fee, many times the average wage of ten cents an hour for people fortunate to have a job. But Andrew earned the money honestly. He was the only man in the entire area who had the expertise needed to dig a well to the depth necessary to reach water and to do it safely for himself in the deep confines of the hole.

Andrew would start counting his hourly wage when he left his home. He would converse with the gentlemen he was digging the well for, but, once he put on his hat, gloves, and boots and neared the well, he became serious and totally concentrated on the job at hand.

Andrew stepped inside the large wooden basket and Jacob began to slowly lower Andrew down into the well, carefully lower and lower until Andrew reached the dry floor. Stepping from the basket, Andrew would dig three separate holes around the interior next to the wall, down into the bedrock ground. This was very labor-intensive, time-consuming, often even a suffocating job. Then, he planted three sticks of dynamite into each hole. Next, he would wind the dynamite fuses together and connected them to one long fuse, long enough to reach the surface of the well, and several feet beyond.

Stepping back inside the basket, he would call Jacob and Jacob would slowly but steadily raise him to the surface. Stepping onto the ground, Andrew lit the fuse, then he and Jacob moved several feet from the well. When the nine sticks of dynamite exploded, the ground shook beneath their feet. The windows in the house rattled and smoke billowed from the well.

Three or more days later, allowing time for the air in the well to clear and be safe to breathe again, Andrew entered the well, shoveled the loose dirt into a bucket for Jacob to pull to the surface and empty. This continued until all the loose dirt was removed and he had reached, hopefully, water, but if not, Andrew would again dig three new dynamite holes for the next round of explosions. This was repeated as many times as necessary until a good source of water was reached, ensuring a lasting supply.

Andrew reached water on the second round of dynamite explosions. Water, good, clean, pure water! What a blessing! The most important ingredient needed to uphold human life and here it was readily available. Thank you,

Heavenly Father for the water. Please bless Andrew Taylor and keep him safe.

Irish Blessing

May God give you:
For every storm-a rainbow
For every tear- a smile
For every care-a promise
And a blessing in each trial
For every problem life sends,
A faithful friend to share
For every sigh-a sweet song
And an answer for each prayer

1937

Jacob knew to make the orchard a successful enterprise, he must invest all his time, energy, hard work, and money into it. It would require his heart and soul.

He had worked every day in cleaning land for the orchard, but his progress was too slow for him. At this rate, it would be years before the entire orchard was planted. He wanted to get the land cleared and planted as quickly and efficiently as humanly possible and he needed help to accomplish this. He had recently met a nineteen-year-old man--Tom Surratt--with a wife and infant son, who was homeless and looking for work that would put a roof over his head and food upon the table for his family. Jacob wanted him to help work his land.

Jacob went to the bank to borrow the money to pay Andrew for digging the well, and additional money to build a two-room house to be built on the backside of the farm, near the spring, so Tom's family would have a convenient supply of water.

Jacob also borrowed the amount needed to purchase a small, low box of a used bulldozer, which was needed to remove the ground for a basement under one room of the small house he planned to build for Tom and his family. The basement was absolutely necessary to store canned foods and apples and potatoes during the winter months. Plus, a small dozer was needed to remove stumps and large rocks. It would quickly pay for itself, Jacob reasoned.

Milton Ward highly recommended Joseph Scales, another black neighbor who lived on Greenhill Road, about two miles west of Jacob, to build the two-room house. Joseph was a carpenter by trade and had built several homes in the area and near Mount Airy. His own home was a perfect example of his craftsmanship. His home was a three-level structure, with both back and front screen porches. The ground floor contained five large rooms, and under the steep declining roof was four more bedrooms. A full-size basement, which contained two bedrooms, a large playroom for his younger children, and a room with desks and chairs for each school child to study and do their homework. Joseph was sincere in his determination to give each of his children a proper education and even to send them to college.

Joseph had insulated his entire house with Owens Corning Fiberglass insulation and double pane windows so the house was easy to cool in the summer and warm in the winter. (One of the very few homes in the entire area to have such a luxury.) But, the big attraction of his home was the outside walls. He and his older sons had gathered rocks from the fields near his home. He mixed the cement needed to hold the rocks together forming walls that were unique, eye-catching, and awe-inspiring.

Joseph, Jacob, and Tom had a two-room house built in two weeks.

Jacob and Tom immediately tackled the planting of peach trees on the five acres Jacob had cleared. This was a precise job, for the trees had to be planted in a perfect twenty-foot square. Every row had to be completely straight, and regardless of where one stood in the orchard, he could turn around and around, and every tree was exactly in line. Not a single tree was so much as an inch out of line. Jacob was pleased with their accomplishment.

Next, the two, using both dozer and horses, tackled the remaining acreage. Pastureland, hayfields, cornfields, in addition to the land for more peach trees, kept the men fully occupied, but the dozer and the horses could not remove the largest stumps. These were tackled, one at a time, by digging a hole under the stump, then placing two or more sticks of dynamite into the hole. The explosion would blow the stump apart, even removed some of the thickest roots, but still left a mess to clean up and plenty of small roots to be dug by hand and removed.

Most weeks, after providing wood for the two houses, Jacob had two to four wagon loads of wood to sell. Jacob drove the horses to Mount Airy, where he sold the load of wood for fifty cents to poorer families on the back streets. This money was needed to pay Tom's fifty cents a day salary. Yes, Jacob was generous with Tom; a daily income, plus a free house to live in. But Tom earned the income for he quickly and without uttering a word of complaint, tackled every job Jacob assigned him.

Lena was working eight hours per day at the mill. The handle of the knife made her hand totally stiff and cramped by the end of each day. The job was NOT easy.

Lena's first check and every check thereafter was used for the farm. Her income bought boxes of dynamite, gas, and oil for the dozer, kerosene for the lamps and lanterns, the ten cents daily transportation bus fee, fertilizer by the loads, grass seed, lime to sweeten the soil, peach tree seedlings, plus Tom's salary, the days Jacob had not taken wood to sell, leaving just barely enough of each check to buy a few groceries: mostly pinto beans, flour, fatback meat, a little white sugar, and Jacob's Camel cigarettes.

- *An old North Carolina store similar to the old country store in our area.*

One item Jacob purchased which immediately benefited the entire family was a large used "ice box". The heavily insulated metal container was placed on the far end of the back porch where the box was shaded from heat of the summer sun by the large pear tree several feet east of the porch. (Ice wasn't needed during the cold weather.)

Oh, how good COLD milk tasted! How convenient to no longer place covered jugs of milk into buckets, and then lowering the buckets several feet down into the well to help keep the milk from rapidly souring. This did not make the milk very cold but preserved it for two to three days if needed to be kept for that length of time. However, the buckets had to be drawn to the surface and set beside the well, whenever water was needed for the house, and once all the water was drawn, then the milk buckets were lowered into the well once again. Time consuming!

Plus, the ice box kept cooked foods from spoiling, so Lena need not be concerned for the safety of the food for the next day's table. Thank you, Jesus!

Even the two oldest daughters, Iona and Audrey, had their chores. Each one was assigned her own job. This ensured each one did their work without any arguments or misunderstandings. Their contributions to the family required sweeping the floors each day, washing the dishes after supper, bringing the wood for both cookstove and fireplace from the wagon to the cover of the back porch. All this plus, any schoolwork they brought home during the school year. Even Mabel, age 3, helped to feed the cats and chickens, and bringing in wood to the porch.

Lena worried all this work might be too much for the girls, but she also knew the girls were learning an important life lesson: Everyone had to work to survive. Nothing came free. She also knew they needed to be recognized and appreciated for their contribution to the family, and this she did, every day, to the girls' delight.

1938

"Bring food, bring your families, neighbors, and friends. Come to stay all day. Be here no later than 10 A.M." This was the standing invitation every first Sunday in September. Lena's brothers, Herbert and Dillion had this once-a-year event for their families.

Lena had three older brothers. Willy was the oldest and lived in Winston-Salem. Dillion and Herbert operated two dairies on sharecropper status. The dairies were located about 1 ½ miles from Lena's home, across the Lovill River in Carroll County.

All three men were tall, with blue eyes and auburn colored hair. They were God-honoring, God-fearing family men. Each of them had a keen wit, a contagious laugh, and a spontaneous sense of humor. They were full of energy, life, and the joy of living. They were full-blooded Irishmen through and through.

- *Lena's brother, Herbert Skyes standing on his horse to give everyone a good laugh.*

As dairymen, Herbert and Dillion's day started at 4 A.M. each morning. To milk the cows by hand, clean all the utensils that had been used during the milking, then cleaning the milk barns to prepare for the next milking. Electricity did not come to the area until 1944. Which meant that all the work was labor-intensive and time-consuming. After electricity was available, milking machines were used to reduce some of the manual labor.

Depending upon the time of year, their days were spent plowing huge "bottomland" fields for the planting of corn, doing the actual planting of the corn seed across the innumerable rows in the fields, or cultivating the young corn three separate times to combat the weeds invading the fields, or harvesting the grown corn, ear by ear, all by hand, in late October. Plus, up to 3 times a year, huge hay fields were cut, then turned to help the hay dry. Next, the hay was gathered and stored in the barns' lofts.

The milking stalls had to be kept clean, and the removed cow manure was a perfect fertilizer. It required moving from barns and then spreading over the cornfields and gardens. All very time-consuming work.

In addition to the fieldwork, the brothers often needed to repair or build new fencing. Cows, being cows, were always looking on the other side of the fence at the lush hay and cornfields. We all know "the grass is always greener on the other side." "Rounding up" the cows, getting them back inside the pasture gate, sometimes required several hours. The stubborn animals did not want to return to their green pastures. They wanted to roam free and discover new fields. These rebellions were led by one of the big bulls at each dairy. Those bulls thought of themselves as the masters of the herd, of the dairy, even as the masters of the humans who looked after them and who worked to keep them confined inside the huge, fenced pastures. The pastures were lush and green. The bulls just wanted to show who were the real master of the dairy.

In addition to all the work, the brothers also had to assist in the calf birthing process. This could require several hours and had to be done whether during the day or in the middle of the night, whether hot or freezing cold.

This was the brothers' life. Seven days a week, day after day, week after week, month after month, year after year. This went on all through the thirties and forties.

On Sundays, the brothers still milked the cows two times and cleaned the utensils and barns after each milking. NO outside fieldwork was done on Sundays. The middle part of each Sunday was spent with their families.

Due to the confining labor needed at each dairy, Uncle Herbert decided to give his children (two sons and three daughters) and Uncle Dillion's two daughters a special day; The Sykes' Reunion.

"Come for fun and games." It was fun! Not only for Uncle Herbert's and Uncle Dillion's children, but for everyone who came and took part in the day's activities.

The men played games of horseshoes and taught the teenaged boys the art of throwing the shoes to score a perfect "ringer" every time. The men also played baseball in the fields surrounding the house. They also had horse racing across the pasture. The winner was always proud of his accomplishment. Herbert delighted everyone by standing up in his horse's saddle and riding around the yard several times. He was a sight to see: The horse tall and long-legged, Herbert himself stood six feet two inches in stocking feet and standing in the saddle was simply delightful and breathtaking for all the youngsters, and pretty amazing for most of the adults, too!

The teenaged boys enjoyed catching trout in the swiftly moving section of the river nearly ¼ mile north of Uncle Herbert's house. They would come hurrying back with their string of pan-sized trout. All excited and proud of themselves for their contribution to the coming meal. "Aunt Lena, we've got fish! Will you please cook them for us?

We will clean them. You won't have to clean them, we will," they exclaimed. "Yes, I'll gladly cook them for you," Lena answered, knowing that the fish would only be partly cleaned when the boys delivered them to her, but she was willing to finish the job and cook the fish for the boys.

The long, dirt driveway, from the road to the middle of the farm, where the house sat inside a picket fence, became a racetrack for foot racing.

- The younger kids played inside the fenced yard and on the front and back porches. The girls played with their dolls and took part in games of hopscotch.

- The favorite game of the younger boys was marbles, and competition between them was serious and fierce. For a break from the intense games, the boys would chase each other around the house numerous times.

- The boys ages 9-12, played leapfrog, sack races, and wrestled each other.

- The girls ages 9-12, jumped rope and contests were held to see which girl could jump the most times before getting her feet tangled in the rope. They also took turns on the swing that hung from a high limb on the huge oak tree in the backyard.

- The teenaged boys swam in the river, played softball, and allowed the girls to ride with them on their bicycles as they constantly teased them.

- The teenaged girls walked up and down the driveway as they talked about schoolteachers, other students, and of course, their latest boyfriends.

- It was the responsibility of the boys to wind the numerous pails of water from the well in the backyard. Besides the water needed in the kitchen, at least one bucket of water was needed every hour for all the thirsty kids and adults.

- The boys, especially with their robust activities, visited the water buckets quite often. Their trips, combined with their fun-loving mischievousness, could often result in water battles with each other. Often, the boys' heads and even the necks of their shirts were wet before Lena stepped to the backdoor to put a stop to their mischievous prank.

- The boys' favorite prank was slipping behind the outhouse and silently wait until one or two of the girls had entered. The boys would then slowly and quietly slip to the front of the outhouse, and quickly lock the door on the outside and then, the boys would run away and hide; The girls, on discovering the door was locked would scream and yell repeatedly for someone to let them out!   "We'll murder you when we get out!" they'll loudly yell, as they banged on the door, getting more aggravated the longer they waited for someone to unlock the door. "Let us out, NOW!"

The entire yard and surrounding pasture were alive with laughter, shouts of enjoyment, and busy activities, with everyone participating.

There were always two or three new babies brought to the gathering each year by their eager parents. Everyone, from the oldest adult to the smallest child, took turns "cooing" over the babies and were thrilled when they received a big smile from the infant for their reward. How precious and beautiful the babies were!

The women would all bring a covered basket of food to help supply the table. But there was still much work and time required to feed the families. As the women worked together in the kitchen, they discussed their latest dress, bonnet, and other sewing projects. The women also shared any news about family, friends, and neighbors that they had heard since their previous visit. They laughed and enjoyed the companionship of each other while they shared the kitchen chores. The dinners consisted of a large and delicious variety of food:

- Large platters of biscuits and cornbread, one at each end of the table.
- Meats were stewed beef, fried sliced ham with "red-eyed" gravy, fried chicken, chicken and dumplings, and the fried trout the teenaged boys had provided.
- Bowls of vegetables, green beans, creamed potatoes, platters of corn on the cob, chopped onions and green peppers, sliced cucumbers and tomatoes, and leafy lettuces plus, huge cantaloupe and humongous watermelon slices were enjoyed by everyone.

The children enjoyed milk along with their meals. The adults generally had coffee or large glasses of fresh water from the well. Occasionally, even gallons of lemonade sweetened with honey would be available.

Sugar was in short supply, so, all desserts were made using the least amount of sugar as possible. Dillion and Herbert often gathered wild honey from beehives found in hollow trees in the woods surrounding the dairies. This honey was used to sweeten peach, sour cherry, apple pies, and cobblers. Small fried pies made with dried apples were often available.

At 12 o'clock "on the dot" dinner was called for all. "Come and get it" did not need to be repeated.

With everyone gathered around and holding hands, a blessing was said over the table. First, was a request for health of each child, then for the well-being of each adult.

Then, praises of thanksgiving were offered to God for all the many blessings He bestowed upon the families, for His Grace, His Love, and for His Precious Son, Our Lord and Savior, Jesus Christ.

With hearts full of gratitude and empty bellies silently screaming for food, the meal was served.

- First, the plates for the younger children were prepared for them and carried to the back porch where they could eat at the small tables readied for this very use.

- Next, the plates for the larger boys were loaded and carried to the front porch where the boys sat in chairs, the swing, on the steps, and along the edge of the porch.

- All the teenagers carried their plates to the table behind the house or sat on a quilt spread on the ground near the river.

- Next, the men sat down at the table to eat. The women continued to serve everyone, as many wanted "second helpings" of their favorite dish or dessert. Most everyone wanted refills of their beverages. Finally, the ladies were free to sit at the table and enjoy their meal in leisure. The food was delicious, the "company" cordial, and everyone enjoyed themselves.

As soon as the meal was over, the children resumed their various games. After the women washed and dried the dishes and returned them to their proper places, they joined the men where they sat and talked under the oak tree. They all joined together in singing old Irish songs as Grandpa played his fiddle. Dillion and Willie played their guitars. Most of the songs were accompanied by Herbert dancing the Irish Gig. Standing tall, arms at his side, only his feet moving to the rapid beat of the music. He danced many of the songs played. Nearly everyone, the children, teenagers, even adults joined in the dancing, but Herbert outlasted, outperformed ALL of them, and seemed to never grow tired of the music and dancing.

Finally, at nearly 4 o'clock, Jacob was able to get Herbert's attention and off to the empty living room, they retired for a game of checkers. Checkers was Jacob's favorite pastime. Both men took the game very seriously. To both men, it was a game of wits and strategy. Each man was determined to win every game. There was no "give" on the part of either one. Lena often joked that when they were playing checkers, "the house could burn down around them, and they would not even notice it".

- At 5 o'clock, Lena would walk to the living room and say to Jacob, "Herbert is getting a late start to milking. The cows have gathered at the barn and are waiting to be fed and milked, and we need to get home to milk our cow too." Jacob did not even hear her.

- At 5:30, Lena would return to Jacob, "Dillion and the boys have gone ahead and milking the cows and they need Herbert's help. It is getting late, and we need to get home to take care of our animals." Jacob would grunt in agreement, as he continued to play.

- At 6, there was Lena saying," Jacob! Jacob! All the other families have gone home. We need to get home, too. The girls are tired and need to be put to bed." Jacob would reluctantly reply, "Okay, okay, just one more game."

- At 7 o'clock Lena said, "Jacob, come on! By the time we get home and get all the outside work done it will be 9 o'clock. The girls are stretched out on the floor sound asleep, let us go!"

Finally, Jacob would respond to Lena's pleas and slowly stood up and walked away from the checker game. He and Herbert would stretch their backs and arms, and firmly pat each other's backs as they laughed. The tension of the games was finally broken. They were feeling jubilant. Especially the one who had won the most games that evening. The winner would whoop and laugh, feeling brilliant and victorious in defeating his brother-in-law.

This was the exact pattern of all the Sykes' Reunions during the 1930s and 40s.

UNCLE HERBERT

Callie was a beautiful nineteen-year-old when Herbert met her. Callie had a ready smile, a contagious laugh, and engaging personality. Herbert fell totally in love with her the moment they met. The feeling was reciprocated, for Herbert was splendid looking with a charismatic personality and wicked sense of humor. The attraction between them was dynamic and magnetic. They were perfect for each other.

They were only able to see each other occasionally, but their love blossomed and their mutual desire for each other grew to fever pitch. As the weeks turned into months, Herbert walked the floor many restless, sleepless nights. He played sad, soulful songs on his guitar, and became more silent and depressed each day. The longer they were apart, the more weight he lost.

"Lena," he'd gloomily tell her, "Don't fall in love, it'll eat you alive and leave you only a shell of a person!"

You see, Callie was married, and in 1922, no wife left her husband for another man, regardless of how bad her marriage was or how desperately she wanted to be with her new love. It simply was not done. The shame and disgrace would be too great for her and her family to bare. She had no choice but to stay with her husband.

- *A 36' Ford similar to the one Herbert had.*

Callie's husband, Jack, was a nasty-tempered, possessive bully of a man. When he heard the rumor that Callie was seeing another man, he became so enraged at her denials, he locked her in their bedroom where he often struck her and repeatedly, brutally used her, even though by now, she was six months pregnant with his child.

Inside the prison of her room, Callie endured two weeks of this torture before she was finally able to raise the window high enough to slip through. She ran nearly a mile to the nearest neighbor and requested him to notify Herbert where she was and for him to come and get her.

Both Herbert and Jack owned Ford T-model pick-up trucks. Callie and Herbert had just left the neighbor's house when Jack drove up, holding a shotgun out the truck window. Both T-models were pushed to their limit, as Herbert drove to get away and Jack drove to catch up. The narrow dirt road was hilly, rough, cracked, and on Jack's third attempt shooting at them, he lost control of his vehicle, drove off the embankment, down the hill, rolling over and over, instantly killing him.

Herbert and Callie married a few days before the birth of her baby, despite the scandal that lasted for months because Herbert wanted the child to have his name.

Herbert raised Callie's daughter as his own and they had four more children together and a good marriage which lasted the rest of their lifetime.

1939

By the fall of 1939, Lena had been working nearly four years. The job had paid 10 cents an hour when she started, but now paid 20 cents an hour.

With the money, she paid for additional truckloads of fertilizer and limestone, grass seed by the 25-pound bag to sow the hay fields, pastures, and orchard. She also paid for peach tree seedlings by the dozens. For the family, Lena's money paid for another Jersey cow in order to always have a constant supply of milk, a flock of chickens, and a small building with an enclosed fence to ensure the safety of the chickens, gas and upkeep of the car, kerosene for the household lamps and frequently used lantern, the innumerable items needed for daily subsistence, the necessities for turning the place into an income producing property, and this included Tom's daily wage when Jacob was too busy cleaning land to take a load of wood to Mount Airy to sell.

Even with the increase in her pay, there was barely any money left to purchase the necessities the family needed. There was no money for store bought clothes. There was barely enough for the girls to have two pairs of shoes each year, one for summer, one for winter, and they would be completely falling apart before the next pair was due.

Once again, the well had been getting drier all fall, until by November 15th, it was completely dry. While waiting on Andrew Taylor to have the time to dig the well deeper, Jacob labored each day to bring buckets of water from the spring, so Lena, in a tiny effort to conserve the water for the next morning's breakfast, often went to bed thirsty and dehydrated. Many mornings, she pushed herself just to lift her head from her pillow, much less to get out of bed and start her long exhausting day.

Lena was pregnant again, but she could not slow down. There was just so much that absolutely had to be done, regardless of how she felt.

On a Friday morning in late November, a month before the baby's due date, Lena was so weak and sick, she could not force herself to get out of bed. She had developed a fever, and rapidly became sicker and sicker. Her temperature rose dangerously high and she started convulsing so severely, she was chewing her tongue. She collapsed into unconsciousness.

Jacob rushed Lena to the emergency room at Mount Airy hospital. There, Dr. Britt informed Jacob that his wife was too ill for their care. The nearest hospital that might be able to save her life was at Elkin, North Carolina. With sirens blaring, the ambulance carrying Lena headed there.

At the Elkin hospital, Dr. Nesbitt told Jacob that Lena had "kidney poisoning" and that she and her unborn child were near death. The doctor asked Jacob which life he should work to save. Jacob explained to the doctor that there were three young daughters at home who needed their mother and he needed his wife. He asked the doctor to concentrate on saving the mother.

Jacob walked the hospital floor all night and much of the next day, praying for his wife's safe delivery and return to him and his daughters. There was NO way the family could survive without her. Finally, late the next day, Dr. Nesbitt came to Jacob and reported that BOTH his wife and child, a tiny 5-pound daughter were alive and doing well. Their lives had been saved by the rather "new" antibiotic: Penicillin!

Lena slept nearly 24 hours a day during the first week after the baby's birth. The severe kidney infection and the years of strenuous work had left Lena extremely weak and utterly exhausted. Nurses would wake her at 4-hour intervals so she could nurse the baby and at mealtimes. The nurses were kind and gentle but were very firm that Lena must eat. Lena's fever had broken, and she needed nourishment to regain her strength and recover from her illness.

During the second week, Lena began feeling better and was able to sit in the chair in her room and to hold and nurse her baby daughter. As soon as her baby was fed, Lena would return to her bed completely drained.

By the third week, Lena had gained enough strength that she was able to walk from her room, down the hallway to the bathroom. There, for the first time in her life, she enjoyed the wonders of laying in the tub of warm water. The nurses allowed Lena to lay in the tub for 60 minutes each day. The nurses would check on Lena often, adding hot water to the tub to prevent the water from cooling too quickly.

Oh, the luxury, the wonder, the regenerating properties of lying in that tub of warm water! Lena just wanted to lie in it forever. But, throughout the three weeks, Lena's every waking thought was with her family. She missed them very badly. She just wanted to get well and return to them. Jacob and the girls visited Lena each Sunday. The faces of the girls, eager and excited at visiting their mama and new baby sister, was all Lena needed to continue her recovery.

Lena knew the girls and Jacob were doing okay without her at home. Her mother, Sally, had come to stay with the girls the instant she learned Lena had been rushed to the hospital. Sally was a devoted grandmother. She cooked, cleaned the house, kept the fire burning in the heater in the bedroom, and the cookstove in the kitchen constantly fueled, and the rooms warm. Though Lena knew the family was getting along fine without her there, by the end of the fourth week, she was feeling much better and stronger and was ready to return home to her family.

The only problem was the new baby. The tiny infant had weighed just five pounds at birth. Despite being fed every 4 hours, the baby had lost weight. She now weighed only four and half pounds. Dr. Nesbitt was concerned with the infant's decline. He monitored the baby and ran every test available to him. All of which came back showing that everything was normal. All he knew was that the baby slept very little, cried constantly when awake, was rapidly losing weight, and perhaps even its battle for life.

Dr. Nesbitt stood over the baby observing its actions, the constant turning of its head as if searching for something and opening and closing of its fists as it cried. He recognized that the baby was hungry, in fact, starving. Lena's milk was not providing the nutrition the baby needed to survive and grow. Dr. Nesbitt ordered his nurse to prepare a bottle of Similac (a powdered milk formula) for the infant. The nurse hurriedly mixed one tablespoon of formula into 4 oz. of water until completely dissolved. This was a fairly new and untested infant formula, but Dr. Nesbitt did not have a choice. The infant could not survive at the present rate of weight loss.

The baby latched onto the bottle's nipple and suckled greedily, quickly devouring the four ounces. The nurse held the baby to her chest, patted its back, and received three big burps for her effort. For the first time since its birth, the baby slept four solid hours and woke with a smile. The crying was over, the baby had been starving! Lena's breast milk was too weak to provide nutrition the baby needed to grow. Dr. Nesbitt continued to allow the baby to nurse at Lena's breast for a few minutes every four hours. Then, to continue her feeding with four ounces of the "formula" of Similac mixed with 4 ounces of water. With the infant daughter's improvement and Lena's returning strength, they were both released from the hospital and returned home on December 24th, Christmas Eve.

On the way home, Jacob stopped at Lamb's Drug Store in Mount Airy to purchase a container of Similac. The price was exorbitant! He did not have the funds to purchase even one container! He did, however, buy two glass baby bottles. The baby would simply have to drink cow's milk.

Grandma and the girls had decorated the kitchen and the "front" room for Christmas. Grandma had also prepared a turkey, dressing, and her decadent fruit cake for the Christmas table and Lena's homecoming.

Lena, Jacob, Grandma, and the three older daughters were very thankful to their Heavenly Father for the survival and homecoming of Lena and the new baby daughter from their near-death illnesses. "Thank you, thank you dear Heavenly Father for your Grace, Mercy, and

Love. Thank you, thank you." was the constant thought on everyone's mind, tongue, and heart all through Christmas.

Grandma stayed another two weeks as Lena continued regaining her strength. But her own home needed her, so she returned to them. Lena was so grateful to her mother for her dependability, love, and care of her family during her time of need.

After several days of drinking the cow's milk, the baby became extremely constipated. The infant cried fitfully, constantly twisted and unable to rest with the discomfort of a bloated belly.

Daddy asked Dr. Britt if he knew how to help the baby. First, Dr. Britt thought of Similac, but knew Jacob didn't have the money to buy it. Dr. Britt then suggested mixing a tablespoon of Karo syrup into the cow's milk to see if that would relieve the infant's problem. This "formula" required three days to work, but finally, relief came. The baby was soon happy and growing.

The days passed quickly, and it was soon time for Lena to return to work. The mill allowed exactly three months for maternity leave. Any longer and the employee was automatically dismissed from her job. It had been exactly three months since the morning Lena had awakened deathly sick.

Lena could not risk losing her job. Her income was desperately needed to pay bills. The main one of those debts, and she was glad to pay, was to Andrew Taylor. For while she was hospitalized, Andrew had dug and dynamited the well to a depth of seventy-five feet, where a vein of water was reached and rose instantly forty feet up inside the well. Water! Precious Water! At the forty-foot level, it should hold and hopefully never need to be dug deeper.

Lena and Jacob's fourth child was another daughter, me, Nerina. "I'm sorry, Daddy, I wasn't the boy you wanted so badly."

Thank you, Heavenly Father, for the water, and please continue to bless Andrew and keep him safe. Thank you for Mama's and the baby's safe return home. Thank you.

Hush, Little Baby (song)

Hush. Little baby, don't say a word.
Papa's gonna buy you a mockingbird.
And if that mockingbird won't sing,
Mama's gonna buy you a diamond ring.
And if that diamond ring turns brass,
Mama's gonna buy you a looking glass.
And if that looking glass gets broke,
Mama's gonna buy you a billy goat.
And if that billy goat won't pull,
Mama's gonna buy you a cart and mule.
And if that cart and mule turn over,
Mama's gonna buy you a dog named Rover.
And if that dog named Rover won't bark,
Mama's gonna buy you a horse and cart.
And if that horse and cart fall down,
You'll still be the sweetest little baby in town

1940

Mama's job required she cut the fabric into pieces necessary to make children's clothing the mill produced. The fabric had to be cut precisely and rapidly, which required Mama's total concentration. But, after years of doing this work over and over each and every day, the work became totally automatic and downright boring. As she worked her hands, her mind would be with her daughters, the three oldest at school, the baby with her mother at her home, a mile north of Mama's own house.

Every day she silently talked with her Heavenly Father, asking Him to please watch over her daughters, Jacob, and her mother. "Father, I'm here working, unable to be with my daughters, so please look after them and keep them safe. I give them to you for your safe keeping. Thank you, Father, thank you." was her silent, constant prayer.

When her mind wasn't occupied with her family, Mama thought of her precious mother, Sally. Sally was a petite, extremely shy, sweet natured lady, who loved to spend her days making quilts, and scatter rugs from discarded clothing she had cut into narrow strips to be woven together. She also crocheted bedspreads, and ruffled dollies. All Sally had to do was study a picture of a crocheted piece in a magazine and she could make an exact duplicate. The crocheted ruffled dollies were stiffly starched, then each ruffle was pressed around a drinking glass. When dry, the glasses were removed, and the ruffles stayed in place, standing six inches tall! How beautiful! A real showpiece!

- *Lena's mother Sally, her father James, and her three older brothers right to left, Dillion, Herbert, and William. Lena is setting on her mother's lap.*

Mama understood the reason Sally was so quiet and reserved was from her childhood. You see, Sally had no father! No last name! In the first half of the 1900's, a woman having children without being married to the father was a horrible disgrace!

"Sometimes, the selfish acts of other people can have a devastating effect on other people's lives, so we should always consider our actions and the effect those actions may have on the lives of others," Mama said.

Sally was born in 1872 to Rebecca Ann Brannock. Rebecca was NOT married! Oh, the shame! The disgrace! The horror of being born to an unwed mother! How degrading to not have a father, or a home to call their own. Sally just wanted to hide from the world. Sally could not endure the stares, the snickers, the whispers behind hand-covered mouths each time she ventured outside her door.

Rebecca, her mother, was a very attractive teenager when she met an older James Jesse Lundy, the Surry County constable. Shortly thereafter, Rebecca became pregnant. Rebecca's parents, Samuel and Regina Brannock, a highly respected family in the community, raised their granddaughter, plus the six sons and daughters Rebecca had during their 12-year affair: Morgan, Weldon, Isaac Reid, John, Curtis Charles, Sally Ann, and Amanda. The Brannocks provided the home, food, clothing, and education for all seven children.

To make the affair between Rebecca and James even more appalling, James was a married man and his own wife gave him seven legitimate children during the same time: Berthina (Betty), William (Chap), Benjamin, Clayton, Celia, Forester, and Rosina.

Sally was so embarrassed by and ashamed of her mother and the deplorable circumstances of her own birth that she kept her head lowered and her eyes downcast on the rare occasions she ventured outside her home.

She became a recluse in the home of her grandparents. She could not endure the disgust, the contempt, the-know-it-all smirks in people's eyes whenever she left her self-imposed prison.

However, her grandparents insisted Sally accompanied them to church each Sunday. It was there she met James Henry Sykes.

James was a "full-blooded" Irishman, both in spirit and actions. He was six foot tall, handsome, fun-loving, warm hearted. James had a spontaneous personality and wit. He loved the shy, petite Sally from the moment he laid eyes on her.

Many Sundays of patient courtship were required of James before Sally could respond to his attention. James slowly, gently, and lovingly convinced Sally of his love for her, and the circumstances of her birth were NOT important to him.

At the age of 21, Sally married James. To the credit of James, he never once mentioned the subject of Sally's birth to her. With James' love, support, and approval, Sally was finally able to forgive and forget the shame and disgrace that Rebecca had afflicted upon her parents and her siblings as well as herself.

"I might have been able to understand one mistake and one child, but to continue the affair and give birth to seven children with a married man when all along he stayed with his wife and had seven legitimate children with her!"

When Sally stopped to reconsider, she realized that the truly selfish one of the disgraceful affair was James Lundy. Rebecca was a teenager when the two met. Lundy had a respectable job, a wife, and an infant son. Yet, he slipped around to secretly visit Rebecca. He got her pregnant and continued the affair until she had six more children.

James Jesse Lundy was the selfish one. His selfish actions made victims of his wife and her children, Rebecca's parents, Rebecca and her children by his selfishness. Why would any man do this to so many people? Why?

Sally never learned the answer to her question.

"Yes," Mama thought, "Selfish actions can result in a lifetime of damage to other people. So, always consider the consequences of your actions."

Lundy and his wife Sarah raised two of Rebecca's boys. Lundy took his "pick" of the boys, the cutest, most intelligent, giving them his name, home, and education. But this only caused more friction between the two families.

- Lundy's children did NOT appreciate the two boys moving into their home, taking up their space, table, beds, and sharing their clothes, books, and receiving attention from their daddy!

- Rebecca's five remaining children felt left behind, even inferior, because they were not good enough for Lundy to choose them.
- Two more energetic boys only added to Sarah's workload, leading to extreme resentment and frustration on her part. How much more could Lundy ask from her?
- Rebecca's parents did not approve of Lundy "picking" his choice of the children to raise and leaving the other five behind without his attention and concern. Rebecca's mother thought he should have taken all seven or left all seven with her, where they were treated with love and respect.
- The two Brannock boys, as active and intelligent as they were, had to endure slurs, insults, even daily "roughing up" by the larger Lundy boys, every time their mother was busy and not paying close attention to the boys. Rebecca's boys accepted the abuse, knowing to tell Lundy about it, would only result in more "roughhousing" for them.
- However, the Brannock boys' sense of humor, their cleverness, their resourcefulness, saw them through the rough days, and within several months, the entire Lundy family's resentment was replaced with admiration, friendship, and acceptance and then with genuine love for the boys by the entire Lundy family.

The war was over between the boys, and they gradually became the best of friends – even true brothers -- to both family's amazement and gratitude. Thank you, Heavenly Father.

In the meantime, Rebecca Brannock aged 35, met and fell in love with William Copeland, aged 39. They were wed on April 27, 1888, in Dobson, North Carolina. They had a happy marriage, and Rebecca gave birth to two more children: John and Amanda Copeland.

Rebecca, after the birth of Amanda, became ill, gradually getting sicker and sicker until she passed away. William was grieved at the loss of his sweet Rebecca, only his two beautiful children kept him going during his time of grief.

ORCHARD

The land for the orchard was finally ready for the final acreage to be planted in peach trees. In 1937, Daddy had planted five acres as soon as he had the land cleared and sown in grass. The small trees had responded robustingly to the sunshine, rain, and rich soil. They had produced a crop this August, and family, friends, neighbors, and church members had come to the farm and together had purchased the entire crop!

During the fall of 1939, with him and Tom working side by side, they had planted another five acres of trees. By now, the entire farm looked like a feature out of the Progressive Farmer magazine. The pastures were a lush green, the hay fields planted in orchard grass, fescue and alfalfa stood tall and gently swayed with the breeze coming from the blue mountains.

Jacob really enjoyed the beauty of the place, as he looked over the fields to the blue mountain, his heart was full of Praises and Gratitude to his Heavenly Father. Thank you, Father, he rejoiced over and over.

Now, the remaining twelve acres were ready for the Alberta seedlings that had arrived. Alberta was by far the best seller and the buyer's favorite. For the peaches were juicy, golden with a red blush, had cling-free seeds, and absolutely delicious, making it perfect for eating fresh, for pies, preserves, and especially for canning.

The work had proceeded perfectly the first week, for Daddy and Tom seemed to know what the other was doing and then matched his actions perfectly.

On Tuesday of the second week, Daddy stepped on a fist sized rock that rolled under his foot throwing him off balance, onto his back, landing him on the iron pick of his mattic. The pain between his shoulders was instantly excruciating, leaving Daddy unable to move.

Tom extremely concerned for Daddy and his pain, slowly, carefully, helped Daddy to his feet, then they walked slowly to the house, often stopping so Daddy could catch his breath, leaving trees, tools, and everything exactly where they laid.

At the house, Daddy carefully removed his work shirt, washed his face. He then allowed Tom to wash his back. Slowly and painfully, Tom helped Daddy to put on a clean shirt. Daddy didn't know what he had done to his back, he just knew he had to get to Dr. Richard's office as soon as possible, for there was NO way he could make it through the night with this intense pain, not to mention the coming days.

Tom didn't have a driver's license, but Jacob couldn't have cared less, he was in so much pain. Tom, very carefully, drove Jacob to Dr. Richard's office, which was upstairs over a dress shop on Main Street in Mount Airy.

After a brief examination, Dr. Richard, a chiropractic doctor, informed Daddy he had a slipped disc between his shoulder blades. Then, with firm, precise manipulation of the spine, Dr. Richard slipped the disc back into its proper place. Instantly, Daddy's pain was gone and he could take a deep, pain-free breath.

Dr. Richard securely wrapped a long strip of gauze around Daddy's chest and back, in effort to hopefully keep the disc from slipping out of place again.

Knowing he and Tom would need additional help in setting out the last peach trees, he, on the way home, stopped at Milton's store to inquire if he knew anyone in the neighborhood who he might employ to help finish planting the orchard.

Milton replied, "The only man I know you might get to help you is Robert Green. He lives at the end of Greenhill Road, down next to Johnson's Creek. He has a tobacco farm there and he stays busy, but you might get him the days he's not working his own fields. He's a real worker, you'd do good to get him."

Daddy drove to Robert's house, where he was surprised to find Robert at his home, not out in the fields working. Robert informed Daddy he could help him as he had a few days free of tobacco work. Due to the heavy rainfall of the last week, the tobacco plants had taken a second growth and were now producing very large dark green leaves that needed time to mature before they could be harvested.

With Daddy moving slowly and carefully, not wanting to reinjure his back again, Robert's help proved invaluable.

Robert was a tall, black man, very slim, and nearly deaf, but he possessed a positive "can-do" attitude. He worked at a steady pace, all day long, stopping occasionally only for a drink of water or thirty minutes for a quick lunch. He was able to accomplish more in a day than any three ordinary men could.

The three of them, Robert, Tom, and Daddy had the remaining trees set in the ground within days.

Daddy was finally able to take a huge sigh of relief. Now, the orchard was completed and would produce the income needed to give his family a good life.

All this, plus Robert was an expert at the game of checkers. Oh boy!

1941

We lived in a beautiful home, with huge green front and back yards. Against the house on the left was the start of the peach orchard and on the right, the driveway and a huge garden.

The house contained 5 large rooms, with both front and back covered porches. The back porch was used every day, almost as an extended work and storage room. The front porch was used every summer evening after supper as a refuge from the overheated house.

The home, as with all frame houses built in the early 1900's, had no insulation. Strong gusts of wind blowing from the mountains, blew right through the walls and down from the attic and made itself to home, and at times it would blow night and day for several days at a time.

The curtains would gently billow away from the windows almost ghost-like. A room without a fire in the wood burning heater was uncomfortably cold. The water in a bucket needed to prepare breakfast, would freeze solid, and had to be placed on the cookstove once the fire was burning---a 4 AM necessity—to slowly defrost.

Each one in the family wore two shirts, plus a sweater, and jacket. The girls wore two cotton slips under their long sleeve dresses, plus two pair of socks pulled as high as possible, all in an effort to keep warm in the house.

The only way to get truly warm during bouts of 25 degrees or below weather was to "crawl" into their beds, lay back-to-back, feet to feet under several quilts. Finally, warm and comfortable, they slept soundly.

When the winter days were cold, and we complained about being cold, Daddy would tell us about the coldest winter he and his family endured. As a young man raised on a farm, he could take the winter however they came, but the winter of 1919 was a different matter.

The weather turned cold in early December and stayed cold throughout the coming 3 months. The trouble began with the first snowfall. It fell on a ground already frozen, and with the following days staying cloudy and cold, with no sunshine to melt the snow, the snow froze solid. Each new snow fell on the hard frozen snow, and it quickly froze solid also. This repeat snow and freeze reached 3 feet, 4 feet in places, of solid frozen white ice, that was impossible to walk on! It wasn't long before the family was in trouble. They did not have sufficient wood at the house for the fireplace or the cookstove. It was almost impossible to walk on the frozen surface to get to the barn to milk the two cows and feed the horses. To make matters worse, the roof was cracking, indicating the roof might be ready to cave in. If all this wasn't enough, there was not sufficient coats or quilts to keep the family warm when the weather was this COLD!

Jacob, 19, was teaching school in Patrick County. The winter was harsh there also, making it impossible for Jacob to travel home to help his family.

However, the three siblings under him, Effie, Bertie, and Claude tackled the frozen snow. Effie and Bertie were pretty and petite, but that didn't slow them down, they stayed with their brother every minute he ventured outside. Each one wrapped in layers of clothes, plus hats, scarves, and mittens. Outside, they tied a rope around each one's waist to stay connected if one should fall. They sat on old buckets and pushing with their feet, managed to move across the back yard. At the barn, they tied another longer rope from the barn, to the well, back to the house and with an additional rope from the porch to the outhouse. This enabled the three by holding the ropes to move safely from one section to the next.

Mornings required 2-3 hours to milk the two cows, feed the horses, chickens, cats, and dog in the barn and to bring several buckets of water from the well, and several snow sleds of wood for the cookstove and the 2 fireplaces that were kept burning 24/7, when it was this cold outside. Another 3 hours each afternoon, to repeat the same chores.

Concerned for the roof's stability, under the heavy weight of snow and ice, the 3 tackled the dangerous job of snow removal. They were hoping to save the roof and prevent the "all too real" possibility of it craving in on the family below.

Standing on the ground, they used ordinary garden rakes to pull the snow and ice from the lowest edge of the roof on both sides of the house. Next, taking turns, each stood on the lower rungs of the ladder and, again using the rakes, pulled another row of snow from the roof. Then, Claude, working along this time, climbed the ladder and removed a third row. Next, Claude cautiously, stepped from the ladder onto the roof and sat down. With the girls pushing and Claude pulling with all his strength, the ladder was raised, then lowered flat onto the roof. Claude returned to the ladder and continued with the removal. This time, pushing the chunks of snow and ice away and down the roof to land next to the house. This was extremely slow moving, but sufficient snow and ice were removed between each snowfall, that the roof was able to endure the weight.

On each removal of the snow, a 2- or 3-inch layer of snow was left on the roof's surface to help prevent damaging the surface, which could cause the roof to start leaking.

As Claude worked along on the roof, the girls worked to remove the chunks of frozen snow rapidly accumulating next to the house to help prevent the family from being blocked inside! The girls dragged the sled to the chunks of ice, then rolled them onto the sled. Pulling the sled slowly to prevent falling, they dragged each load of chunks across the nearby driveway and dumped them into the resting garden on the other side.

After EACH new snow, this was a required job and kept the 3 teenagers completely and totally occupied during the middle of each day between their regular chores of tending the animals and bringing in the wood and water.

The siblings enjoyed the companionship of working together. They were proud of providing for their family and appreciated everyone's "Thank You" each night.

However, there was one task that absolutely had to be done---a task the siblings detested, but absolutely without complaining—emptying the 2 nearly full urinals twice a day into the outhouse!

Finally, the snow stopped, the sun brought warmer weather, and the white ice gradually melted, leaving deep mud everywhere to slowly dry.

The family praised the Lord for His Goodness and Mercy which had allowed the family to survive the winter of 1919!

5 PM NEWS-1941

For the past two years, the battery radio had reported on the local 6 P.M. news, that a war was raging in Europe. Hitler, and his highly-trained and equipped Nazi regime, had invaded nine countries killing thousands, leaving each area they waged through totally devastated. But, the news seldom mentioned what Hitler was doing to the Jewish people living in those countries, or what he had done to them in his own country.

The Jewish people from all these countries, men, women, and children, were removed from their homes, and sent to labor and concentration camps. From there, these half-starved men and boys, were used to build huge and deep underground caves and tunnels to house soldiers and to store war supplies, weapons, and even tanks. These men and boys were starved, overworked, and beaten should they fail to accomplish the job allotted to them each day. As the Jewish workers died - their naked, "skin and bones" bodies were simply thrown into a huge hole with hundreds of other dead Jews, and quickly replaced by another Jewish prisoner.

Oh, the Jewish people were God Almighty's Chosen People. How could this be happening?

Then on December 7th, the war was brought to America. Japan, Germany's ally, attacked Pearl Harbor, killing 2,300 soldiers and destroying 188 ships and aircraft, all without warning and while peace negotiations were still apparently ongoing.

President Roosevelt had been preparing for the war, training men, making uniforms, weapons, parachutes, and the millions of items the men would need, plus planes, ships, submarines, tanks, EVERYTHING necessary to fight and win at war. The surprise attack caused the president to declare war and enter it with the equipment that was available.

That included Daddy's younger brother, Aubrey, to be drafted into the war.

"Oh, please, Dear Father in Heaven, keep him safe." Daddy prayed many times every day and night.

PEACHES

The first trees near the house produced a second abundant crop of large, juicy, delicious peaches. Family, friends, and church members again bought the entire crop.

When the first five acres had started blooming and baring fruit, Mr. Eric Hickman, who lived near Winston-Salem, inquired of Milton, if he knew anyone locally who might allow him to place beehives for the summer on their place. He wanted the hives near fruit trees and also near woods for the sourwood blooms. Milton told him about Daddy and his place.

Daddy assured Mr. Hickman he was perfectly welcome to set his hives on his place. Mr. Hickman brought five hives the first summer and placed them on the right of the driveway between the garden and woods, in easy sight for Daddy to keep an eye on.

Daddy was glad to have the bees on his place. They helped to pollinate the peaches and the large garden, and in addition, Mr. Hickman would give the family a gallon of the pure, raw, honey each fall, when he came to remove the hives back to his place for the winter.

When the second five acres started blooming, Mr. Hickman brought an additional five hives. Then, with all 22 acres planted, he increased the hives by ten more.

The entire family loved the honey. It was delicious when placed on hot biscuits, used as a replacement in Mama's desserts and especially in her War Cake she baked. The honey was even more useful when mixed with an equal amount of "white lightening" liquor. The two together soothed a sore throat, eased coughs and chest congestion by sipping a teaspoon at a time and holding in the back of the mouth as long as possible. With no money for doctor visits, home remedies were an absolute necessity, and this one really worked.

IONA

Iona, now fifteen, could be very insistent when it came to something she really wanted, and she truly wanted the front room fashioned into a nice and welcoming living room.

"When we visit our cousins and their parents, they ALL have nice living rooms to welcome their guests, and its only right that we should have a nice living room to welcome guests to our home. Besides, I might get a boyfriend someday, and he will need a place to sit." She repeated to Daddy several times each day.

So, after the peaches were sold, and to please Iona, Daddy took her to Brannock Furniture store and allowed her to pick out the furniture she wanted. She chose a maroon couch with small, light blue flowers, and two light blue chairs with small, maroon flowers, four end tables and three woven scatter rugs. She was pleased with what she had chosen, then she spotted a four- foot-tall Victor Victorian hand-cranked phonograph record player, which included a dozen of the latest forty-five records!

She had to have it! All of it! "This would make a perfect living room," she told Daddy, "And we'll even have music to enjoy and dance too."

Iona was exuberant, and Daddy was relieved from her constant nagging, but he had less money to pay on debts. In addition to his money concerns, Daddy's back was still giving him a lot of pain in spite of his frequent trips to Dr. Richards.

On his last visit, Dr. Richards made a halter for Daddy to use to help relieve Daddy's back pain. The halter was made with narrow strips of soft leather which fitted around his head and under his chin. From the top of the halter, a leather strap was screwed securely into a 2x4 timber over the ceiling of the back porch. Daddy was to fit his head inside the halter, then let his entire weight hang by his neck. This lifted the body's weight from his back, pulled the vertebrae into place, and gave Daddy relief from the pain. By doing this exercise regularly, the vertebrae is kept in its proper place, constantly - so hopefully - heal itself.

But the thing that worried Daddy the MOST was Alberta peach orchards were being set out in Patrick, Carroll, and Surry Counties. One of these orchards contained 40 acres, and was just five miles north of Daddy's place.

Yes! Daddy wasn't the only one who read the Progressive Farmer and then took their advice!

SCREAM

Mama screamed! Mama was standing at the kitchen door. She screamed again, even louder! What was going on? Was a monster coming in the door? Was he about to grab her and eat her? I ran to her. I would protect her! She suddenly ran to the far end of the back porch. There daddy was hanging himself! NO! NO! Mama and I both screamed as Mama wrapped her arms around Daddy and tried to lift him up. I hugged one of his legs, trying to lift it! Daddy started struggling to free himself, Mama and I held on tighter, determined to lift him to stop the hanging, and killing himself! Daddy struggled, we held tighter!

Daddy finally struggled free from our arms and the halter. "Stop! Stop!" he commanded. "What are you doing?" Mama hysterically asked him.

"I told you last week that Dr. Richard's was making a halter for me. By using this halter, it takes the pressure off my slipped vertebrae, and this will give me relief from my pain." He said, "I'm not hanging myself. I'm only following Dr. Richard's instructions."

Mama, slowly regained control of her emotions," Oh Jacob, oh Jacob. I'm sorry. It looked like you were hanging yourself! You know how I couldn't make it if something happened to you!" she whispered.

Mama and Daddy held each other tightly as they slowly calmed down.

Then to my amazement, they both started laughing. They laughed, and laughed, and continued to laugh until both collapsed into kitchen chairs.

"Boy, mamas and daddies can sure act silly, sometimes." I thought

FRONT PORCH

Our only relief from the heated house those days was our escape to the front porch. Starting in early June until early October, after supper each evening, the front porch was our refuge, and our place to bond closer and truly enjoy each other's jokes, stories, and the songs we sang together.

Daddy and Mama sang songs from the Primitive Baptist Hymnal, and Old Irish Songs that could be very sad, even mournful. Daddy told us about his childhood at home, school, and activities with the neighborhood children on Sunday afternoons. Daddy's stories were interesting and entertaining, and I never tired of listening to them, regardless of the number of times we asked him to tell them again.

He told us a mystery and offered no solution: On a level spot of ground between our house and the spring was a decaying one-room log cabin. The roof had fallen to the ground. Daddy and Tom had removed the remnants of the logs and sawed them into wood for the heater.

Next, they removed the chimney rocks and all the bushes, vines, and debris around the old home, leaving only the fireplace hearth to be removed. The large flat rock of the hearth was so heavy, only the horses could drag them away.

On the ground where the hearth had been, Daddy noticed something white in the dirt. Bowing down, Daddy moved some of the dirt – it was a BONE! Digging deeper and wider, more and more bones were found and removed. It was a human skeleton! Who – why – would anyone bury a body under a hearth? Why the secrecy? Why wasn't the body buried in the ground with a marker at the head of the grave? Had this person been murdered, and the body hidden?

Daddy reported the finding to the Patrick County Sheriff. The sheriff told Daddy he had no way to determine the who, why, or when behind the bones. The sheriff, however, was certain the bones were a woman's skeleton about 5' 4''. The bones were still strong after being buried for so long, so she must have been young and healthy. That's all Daddy ever learned about the victim, but Daddy did think about the circumstances of her death, many times during the following years.

CORN SHUCKING

Daddy told us one of his favorite activities growing up was the November corn shucking parties his family and five other neighboring families participated in each year. Each family pulled their field corn, then hauled the corn to the far end of their back yard to be shucked. Shucking corn was an easy job, but VERY time consuming. The neighbors' entire families would gather at one of the participating homes around 2 p.m. – on a Friday when it was not raining or too cold and windy.

Everyone brought extra coats and wraps, old chairs to sit on, and plenty of food to accompany the host's supper. Everyone stayed until ALL the corn was shucked and stored in the corn bin. Everyone gathered all the way around the large pile of corn, and worked steadily until 5 P.M., supper time. By now more people had arrived, some to help shuck, some to keep the readied corn moved to the bin, some to build a large fire so everyone had a place to warm, and some with musical instruments to provide entertainment, and one or two of the men always arrived with a couple of jugs of homemade "white lightening".

By 8 P.M. the party (?) was lively and spirited. Children were running around the corn pile and the huge fire, fully enjoying themselves. The fire was steadily growing bigger and bigger and hotter, the laughs more often and louder, the music faster and jollier, (sad, slow songs were over), the men tipsier and more jovial, their jokes raunchier, and the huge pile of corn was rapidly shrinking. The job was usually accomplished by 10 P.M. to midnight at the latest, but EVERYONE stayed until all the corn was shucked and most of the children sound asleep.

MOLASSES

Another yearly job, Daddy told us, was molasses making. Molasses is a delicate tasting sugar substitute that contains iron, sulfur, and other minerals. It was totally delicious and energizing.

The sorghum sugar cane looks like corn, only smaller and more delicate and was planted and cultivated the same as corn. One-fourth acre was planted each year in June and needed to be harvested before the first frost. One-fourth acre would produce 10 to 15 gallons of syrup and would require 10 to 12 hours of cooking until the thin green juice was cooked to a beautiful brown syrup, the consistency of honey.

First the cane was cut down using a machete, six inches above the ground and laid in piles every six to eight feet apart. Next, one cane at a time, the leaves were pulled away to later be fed to the cows. The triangle seed head was removed with a large knife, then placed into bags or boxes to be later dried for grinding into flour. The stalks were moved to the grinder.

The stalks, five to six at a time, were fed into the grinder. The horse pulled the grinder by circling around, around and around it, extracting the thin green juice, which flowed into a large clean bucket below for collection.

The cooking pit was surrounded on three sides by flat rocks until they reached a three-foot high and six-foot-long base. Then a stainless-steel pan of the exact measurement was laid on the rock foundation. One end of the pit was left open to feed wood to the fire underneath. A twelve foot six-inch-tall stove pipe was connected to the opposite end of the pit up through the roof to ensure the pipe had good drawl, and smoke removal.

Each full bucket was rushed to the cooking pit, where it was first strained to remove any debris that might have fallen into it. The fire underneath the pan was started and as more buckets of syrup was poured into the pan, the fire was kept at a steady burn, not too hot, not too cold. From the first bucket of juice until the tenth, (or more), the syrup had to be stirred constantly. The stirrer looked something like a long-handled hoe, and stirring syrup was its ONLY usage. As the syrup started to simmer, foam began to gather on the surface of the syrup. The foam had to be swiftly and continuously removed. The fire, the stirring, the skimming, all had to be done the entire time which required ten to twelve hours of cooking. Finally, the syrup was reduced and then dipped and poured into one half gallon canning jars, which were stored inside the pantry, located in a bedroom of the house.   This was, at the very best, a two-day job, if the entire family pitched in and done their share, which meant no school for the older children, just as nearly ALL the jobs on the farm required.

1942

By May 1st, the orchard was in full bloom due to the unusually warm weather of March- the entire area was a breath-taking pink - so pretty with the blue mountains as a backdrop. The place looked like an artist painting.

Listening to the weather forecast on the battery radio, Daddy learned there was a severe nor'easter coming our way, bringing 25-degree temperatures, winds, and maybe even some snow.

"Oh, Lord, no, please," Daddy groaned, knowing this would destroy the coming crop of peaches.

The two days before the freeze was to arrive, Daddy and Tom took the horses and wagon and frantically gathered the used, wore out, tires from behind Milton's store and discarded tires laying in the edge of the woods along the road where neighbors had thrown them. In the orchard the tires were set three or four at a time, with a small armful of kindling wood under each pile. Then both were sprinkled with kerosene to ensure a quick burn. The tire piles were placed every 15 feet apart, and there were sufficient tires to cover the first 5 acres of fruit trees.

Daddy hoped and prayed the heat from the burning tires and the heavy, thick smoke this would produce, would warm the air surrounding the trees to keep the freeze from killing the tiny peach inside each bloom.

Dad and Tom stayed with the trees starting the first afternoon of the coming freeze to 36 hours later, to keep the tires steadily burning.

On the third day, after all the tires were burned, the freeze moved eastwardly, and the sun and warm weather returned. Daddy and Tom walked through the orchard, picking blooms from trees, opening the petals, to find the tiny peach in the base of the bloom: black. BLACK, the peaches had been killed despite their work and effort to prevent this from happening. BLACK! BLACK! Not a single peach would be produced from the 22-acre orchard this summer! The weather had just been too cold!

Two days later, Daddy and Tom gathered to discuss their plans. Both men knew Tom was no longer needed. His work on the place was finished.

Tom told Daddy his wife was wanting to move to Mount Airy, where hopefully they both could get a job at one of the hosiery mills. His wife wanted a car, nice furniture, new clothes, food, everything for a better life and she didn't mind working to help Tom provide for their new lifestyle.

Daddy shook Tom's hand solidly and earnestly, thanked him for his work and wished Tom and his wife the very best. Their working together had accomplished much, but it was time for Tom to move on.

That night, when Mama learned Tom was leaving and she would no longer be required to pay his daily wage, Mama was deeply relieved. This was one demanding expense the orchard would no longer require from her.

TIME WITH DADDY

With Mama at work, and my three older sisters in school, I accompanied Daddy almost every day and everywhere. I was three years old, normal size, energetic and able to follow in Daddy's footsteps everywhere he ventured. The days he worked as a substitute rural mail carrier, I went with him and was allowed inside the post office. I sat on the floor near where Daddy sorted the mail, then placed the mail inside the small slots.

The Mount Airy Post Office was so clean it shined and everyone who worked there was polite and professional. But for the life of me, I could not understand those nice men spitting brown spit into the beautiful small golden bowls sitting on the floor! Men should have better manners than that!

I rode with Daddy, sitting in the backseat among boxes of mail as he made his route. He occasionally stopped to speak to someone at their boxes.

Many days, I also accompanied Daddy as he drove the horses to Uncle Herbert's dairy to get a wagon load of cow manure. The trips to Uncle Herbert's house were quick and easy as part of the road was downhill. I waited and played in Uncle Herbert's yard or back porch as Daddy and he loaded the wagon, one shovel full at a time. This work required three to four hours, but I didn't mind waiting, I loved the outdoors, and Uncle Herbert's place.

The way home was a different story, however. The horses were hardly out of Uncle Herbert's driveway before they needed a break and when we reached the long uphill part of the road, it was a slow progress. It took everything the two mature horses had to pull the extremely heavy wagon twenty feet before needing to stop to catch their breath. Daddy and I stepped from the wagon, in effort to lighten the load a little, but it was still extremely heavy for the horses. I was always glad when we finally reached home, but I think Daddy and the horses were even more relieved!

I accompanied Daddy on his rare visits to the bank, to Dr. Richard's office, to the seed store, and when on the way home, we would stop at Milton's store. Milton and Daddy shared jokes to see which one could make the other laugh the loudest.

But the biggest thrill of all was when Daddy used dynamite to remove the last few huge stumps in the fields north of the house. These fields were used to plant corn to feed the horses, cows, chickens and also to be ground into cornmeal for the family's cornbread.

Daddy dug under each stump, inserted two or three sticks of dynamite, then lit the fuse and hurried over to join me where I stood far from the blast. With my hands over my ears, the explosion was thunderingly loud, blowing pieces of stump and debris far and wide. The smell, the smoke, the sound was wonderfully exciting. I jumped up and down at the wonder of it all!

NORA

One Thursday afternoon, Daddy and I stopped at Andrew's home, and there I met his wife, Nora. Nora greeted me with a huge smile, wide open arms, and I instantly fell in love with her. Nora and Andrew were not blessed with any children of their own, so Nora adopted all the neighbor's children who would allow her this freedom.

Nora was the cook for the First National Bank's president Mr. Sawcett. Mr. Sawcett could afford the best cook available, and Nora was that person. Her meals were delicious and nourishing, her meats were always tender and seasoned to perfection, her vegetables colorful and crisp, her desserts mouth-watering -- but the best part of Nora's meals was her made from scratch yeast rolls. How can words describe the tantalizing aroma, the taste, the fluffiness, of Nora's yeast rolls?

Nora not only prepared breakfast and lunch for Mr. Sawcett and his family, but also for guests and bank investors who visited during lunchtime. Occasionally, Nora had a small amount of rolls left over and brought them home to share with Andrew.

Thursday evenings Nora did not work for Mr. Sawcett as all the stores, including the bank closed at 1 o'clock. The entire town shut down and became a ghost town each Thursday afternoon.

Many of those Thursday afternoons when Daddy substituted as a mail carrier, Nora invited me to spend the time with her, to my delight, until Daddy returned from the route to pick me up.

Even though I was only three to five years old those years, Nora allowed me to use her Stereoscope Viewer 1896, only warning, "Hold it carefully and don't drop it, for if its dropped, it could break, and we don't want that to happen, now do we?" she sweetly said.

Nora gave me complete freedom with the Stereoscope as she went about her housework. The Stereoscope and the one hundred view card collection was fascinating and awe-inspiring to me. The cards showed pictures of buildings, towns, streets, mountains, rivers, and people all over the world! The people, especially in other countries, their faces, their clothes, their homes, their animals. I was totally captivated as I carefully studied the picture each card depicted, and two to three hours would quickly pass before I could view all the cards. "Thank you, Nora."

And I never, not once, dropped the Stereoscope Viewer 1896!

Nora's home was furnished far better than our home. Nora had an upholstered velvet couch with matching chairs in her living room, instead of using the room as a bedroom as was the custom in most homes. Nora's living room even had velvet curtains on the windows and large woven scatter rugs on the floor! Nora had a separate dining room with a huge table surrounded by high-back wooden chairs. Plus, a huge glass door hutch for storing her best dishes. Nora's kitchen had built-in wall-to-wall cabinets. Plus, Nora had her own car and could drive it to work and to church. Nora, her house, her car, and everything about her smelled like yeast rolls and lavender bath powder.

Nora was rich! Absolutely RICH! Yes, Nora was rich, rich in all the qualities that made for a loving, caring human being. She was a true Child of God.

Nora fully believed in eating healthy, staying active, and home remedies. Her favorite home remedy was Bone Broth, which she drank ½ glass per day. The broth was good for hair, skin, joints, energy, and everything in the body, Nora stated. Any leftover meat bone will make a delicious broth, use large beef, pork bones, along with meaty pork ribs, oxtails, neck bones, ham or shank bones, leftover turkey or chicken bones and feet -- use whatever mix of bones you have on hand, she would tell Mama as she shared her knowledge of the wonders of Bone Broth.

1943

During the late fall and early spring, Daddy had spent most of his time in the orchard, doing the time-consuming job of pruning each tree to remove the center growth of limbs. This pruning allowed sunlight to reach the coming years peaches, enabling a uniform ripening and also to limit the number of peaches to a tree ensuring large growth peaches.

Each Saturday morning, with the help of my sister Mabel and me, the limbs were gathered, placed on the wagon and then hauled to the backyard, where Daddy worked them into wood for the heater and my sister and I carried the wood to the covered back porch to ensure the wood would be dry for using in the cookstove.

The spring came late and warm with regular rain showers, resulting in the trees covered in blooms, and a bunker crop of peaches on the entire 22-acre orchard.

Daddy had sprayed the trees three different times with both insecticides to kill insects, and fungicides to stop any leaf damage due to fungi.

Daddy had braced many of the largest tree limbs with two by three-inch wooden props to support the heavy-laden limbs to prevent the limbs from breaking.

Daddy realized more advertising was needed to bring additional buyers to his orchard. He tacked announcements of "Peaches for Sale" in all the area's stores, placed ads in both the Mount Airy News and the Mount Airy Times Newspapers. In addition to the weekly ads on WPAQ radio station. He talked "peaches" to everyone he met as he traveled back and forth: neighbors, people on the streets of Mount Airy, everyone at his church, gentlemen sitting around the wood heater at Milton's store. He even asked Mama to leave announcements all over the mill for the workers to see, and the daughters to take to school and give to the teachers and their friends. He also visited two trucking companies in Mt. Airy who hauled wholesale foods to grocery stores, to see if they could ask store owners to buy his peaches.

By June 15th, everything was ready for the increase in customers Daddy fully believed would come. Everything that is, except the wagon load of wooden peach baskets stored in the two-room house Tom had lived in.

On rainy days during the past year, Daddy and I had assembled the ready-cut wooden pieces together with small nails. I watched Daddy nail the pieces together and kept the next piece within a twelve-inch reach at his ready. Together we could assemble a wooden bushel basket, within thirty minutes.

So now, all that was required was to bring them to the backyard. They were at the disposal of any customers who did not bring their own or for any truckers to load his truck.

Saturday, June 1st, was a beautiful day, clear skies, warm sunshine, sparkling green orchard and fields, and a robust orchard loaded with big, juicy, delicious peaches.

My sister, Mabel and I accompanied Daddy to help load the baskets onto the horse-drawn wagon. The wagon was loaded a good three feet over the bed of the wagon. Daddy, with the horse's reins in one hand, climbed up on the baskets.

The horses were feeling playful and bored from waiting so long, they took off before Daddy had a chance to sit down on the baskets. He was standing on them when the runaway horses turned a sharp curve through a row of peach trees. The baskets shifted, and Daddy fell from the wagon, his elbow landing on a rock. The horses continued their flight.

Daddy lay on the ground for several minutes, the breath knocked completely out of him. Then, he slowly, carefully sat up, holding his elbow. He didn't scream, he didn't cry, he didn't even use foul language, he simply said, "My elbow is broken."

I instantly busted out crying, "I don't want my Daddy hurt! I don't want my Daddy hurt!" I sobbed.

Daddy calmly said to Mabel, "Run to the house and tell Mama I've had an accident, then go to John Worrell's. I need him to take me to the hospital." Then Daddy said to me as Mabel took off running as fast as possible, "I'm okay, no need to cry. Just walk with me to the house."

From the backside of the farm to John's house, was nearly a quarter mile. As Mabel neared our yard, she started shouting to Mama inside the house, "Daddy's hurt! Daddy's hurt!" As Mama came to the backdoor, "I'm going to John's to see if he'll take Daddy to the hospital. If John's not at home, I'll go to Milton's or Andrew's or Kermit's -- somebody, until I get someone to help," she panted as she sped away.

Daddy, after catching his breath, carefully stood up, and with a pale face, white lips and in excruciating pain, holding his left elbow with his right hand, slowly, but steadily, walked to the house and entered the yard as John drove into the yard to meet him.

The horses and wagon, with its load of peach baskets, were resting quietly next to the barn.

At the Mount Airy Hospital on Gilmore Street, Daddy was given medication for the unbearable pain. Then Dr. Britt informed Daddy his elbow was broken into two separate pieces.

Dr. Britt put Daddy's arm in a plaster cast from his shoulder to his wrist. The arm was placed against Daddy's chest, with his hand resting against the right side of his neck.

"Mr. Mosley, I'm sorry to tell you, but your arm is ruined. You'll never be able to move your arm from this position. Your arm will be frozen with your hand at your neck for the rest of your life."

Daddy, despite the wrenching pain, sense of humor kicked into play, and he told Dr. Britt," That's the arm I hug my wife with and I don't aim for my hugger to be ruined."

The next three weeks were a living nightmare for Daddy because the prescription painkiller hardly lessened the pain. But the debilitating pain in Daddy's arm couldn't compare to the pain in Daddy's spirit.

Other than individuals buying 1 or 2 bushels of peaches for their own family's personal use, no merchants, no truckers, no wholesalers, came to buy peaches.

In fact, most of the trees didn't have a single peach picked from them and a full 95% of the crop fell on the ground to lie there and ROT! ROT! ROT!

CHICKENS

Early each spring, Mama would order several dozen baby chicks from a mail order catalog. Two weeks later the mailman would deliver the chicks to our backdoor in square cardboard boxes tied with twine. Nickel-sized holes were punched in the sides and lids of the boxes for ventilation. The chicks arrived healthy and hungry. Mama would immediately place them into large cardboard boxes on our screened back porch. The chicks were provided with water and were fed cornmeal four times a day.

- *Leno's flock of chickens she raised each spring in front of the chicken coop.*

The baby chicks were wonderfully delicate creatures. They were tiny and soft. They snuggled close together and chirped contently as I held the biddies to my chest. I rubbed their soft down; I cooed to them; and fed them from the palm of my hand. Just being near them and watching their enchanting actions filled my heart with joy and made my spirit sing. Oh, how I loved those beautiful babies, and I knew, I just KNEW that they loved me in return.

The baby chicks quickly outgrew the boxes on the back porch, so Mama would transfer them to the chicken house with its tall enclosed wired fence. Cracked corn and fresh water were given to them each day. By the time the chicks were a quarter grown, the door to the chicken lot was left open so they could roam freely in search of bugs, flying insects, grasshoppers, and worms in the barn lot, the orchard, the pasture, and the fields surrounding our house. This helped to satisfy their insatiable appetite.

The favorite place for the rapidly growing chicks was our yard where food was handy and where humans and farm animals provided companionship. The chicks flocked together and what one did they all mimicked as one spontaneous unit.

The young roosters jumped high at each other in mock battles for supremacy. They were territorial and continually chased each other for favorite scratching ground and food. The young cocks fought constantly to be the highest alpha male of the yard. They would fly up and perch on the farm equipment, the wood pile, the fence post, and even the handlebars of my tricycle. They would even attempt to perch on the backs of the horses. Boy, those young cocks loved those lofty thrones.

The freshly laundered bed sheets, hanging on the clothesline and flowing gently in the breeze, were monsters that they pecked at and battled with. The young roosters announced the arrival of visitors and would run to greet them as they entered the yard.

The young cocks had to be shewed from the front porch every day. They particularly loved standing on the top of the porch swing. Their activity would cause the swing to rock back and forth. From this adventurous height, they challenged each other to see which one could fly off the swing and land the furthest from the porch. The cocks determinedly chased after the pullets in an effort to mount them. This sent the pullets squawking and running for dear life. The cocks nursed a personal vendetta against the cat. They would chase her with such a vengeance, that she could only find safety in the branches of the pear tree. Even the old hound dog could not escape their bullying. They would run him from his bed in the shade and claim it as their own.

In eager anticipation of additional food, the chickens would follow closely at our heels whenever we carried a bucket or bag across the yard. They would even peck at my toes as I carried table scraps out to feed the dog. They worked eagerly to steal the scraps from the dog.

Boy, they had turned into MONSTERS!

Every morning at 4:30 a.m. the half-grown roosters would wake everyone in the house with their loud, insistence, awkward attempts at crowing. Pulling the quilt over my head only slightly muffled their hideous racket.

By now, my adoring love affair with the baby chicks was totally and completely over. How could such tiny, precious creatures as the baby chicks become such annoying barnyard "monsters" in such a short period of time?

The entire flock would become excited and run hither and thither whenever a strange dog came nosing around the yard. Or, when a strange tom cat came courting our enticing feline. At night, we were often awakened by the chickens' loud squawks and cries when a strange dog, possum, or raccoon came near their enclosed pen.

The monsters pecked the ripening strawberries and tomatoes. They would jump to peck the peaches on the low heavy-laden limbs. They preferred those peaches to the ones lying on the ground. They scratched up and left ridges in the driveway with their daily sand baths. Those holes resulted in mud puddles when it rained. They even scratched in Mama's neatly planted flower beds!

The entire flock frustrated the cow as they scurried and dashed about her feed box trying to steal her food, while Mama was milking her. The chickens aggravated Daddy's two horses by flying and leaping around their hoofs and legs seeking to find grubs as Daddy plowed the fields. Or, after insects the horses stirred up as they worked the hay fields.

While the chickens were elsewhere pestering the cows or horses, to the delight of the kittens they were able to come out of their hiding places to play, jump, and tumble about. The kittens celebrated their freedom and enjoyed a joyous kitten party, until the chickens returned to the yard and chased the kittens back to the safety of their hiding place under the back porch.

On the rare occasions, when a low flying hawk circled overheard or a black snake crossed the yard, the entire flock would go wild. The chickens could not jump high enough, run in circles fast enough, or squawk loud enough in demonstrating their dismay and displeasure. The chickens would create such a racket, that it would cause the dogs of our nearest neighbor, 200 yards away, to begin to bark wildly. The barking of the dogs would only excite the chickens further. The barking of the dogs would carry from dogs of one neighbor to the dogs of another neighbor until the entire community was in an uproar!

Yes, the chickens were MONSTERS! They ruled the barnyard and were a complete nuisance to the humans and other animals. But, living on a farm in southern Patrick County in the mid 1900's, this was a yearly ritual necessary to provide eggs and meat for the family table. By late winter, the supply would be exhausted, so on April 1st, Mama would again place her order for several dozen baby chicks.

The precious, darling baby chicks which turned into barnyard monsters was an ordeal the family endured each year. But the chickens were angels compared to the two billy goats Mama raised one summer. Those goats really were barnyard monsters.

But even the goats were pleasant and mild mannered compared to the two tom turkeys raised for Thanksgiving and Christmas. The turkeys easily won the first place for being the absolute troublemaking, bullying, terror monsters of the barnyard. Even my big, strong Daddy would take extra steps to avoid crossing their path!

But the one thing the chickens, turkeys, and goats had in common was their love for the fallen peaches on the ground! Boy, how they LOVED them!

SITTING ON THE FRONT PORCH

The entire family escaped the heat of the house every evening after supper, to retiring to the front porch. We watched the sun slowly, slowly sinking lower and lower, turning the sky blues and yellows to a thousand shades of red and gold. Every sunset seemed to compete to be more awesome than the previous evenings. We treasured the beauty as the colors grew darker and deeper until all the sky was completely dark. We sang songs, told jokes and riddles, and Mama and Daddy shared their childhood memories with us. We sat in chairs, in the porch swing, and occasionally even sitting on the edge of the porch, our bare feet laying on the cool gravel against the foundation.

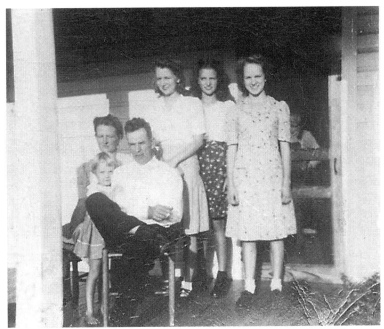

- *Jacob and Lena seated on our front porch with me standing next to daddy. My sisters standing behind up right to left, Audrey, Mabel, and Iona.*

The night came alive with whip-poor-wills, each calling out to his sweetheart. Their call also notified everyone spring had arrived and it was time for farmers to plant their fields of corn. Next came the lightning bugs by the thousands. They filled the night sky like sparkling diamonds. I loved to catch one and hold it close to watch its enticing display. I would open my hand, letting it fly away, then see how long I was able to follow it as it flew into the night. Late summer, the lightning bugs were replaced by millions of fall crickets. The male crickets rubbed their wings together non-stop, filling the woods and entire area with them singing to attract a lover and warn their competitors away. This constant song was totally relaxing and I LOVED to snuggle in bed and fall asleep listening to them.

Occasionally, we watched a thunderstorm as it traveled down the mountainside from east to west, sending flashes of light that lit up the universe for an instant, then was followed by the roaring thunder. The cats and the old dog found us on the porch, and cuddled close for safety those evenings. Even the whip-poor-wills and all the insects were completely silent during a storm. Where did they go? Did they hide? Did they fly away ahead of the storm? I only know they would return after the storm passed to resume their beautiful night music.

Mama could tell the coming weather by the sunset:
Red sky at night, Sailors delight
Red sky at morning, Sailors take warning

QUESTION

Daddy asked me: "What's black and white and red all over?" I offered a number of suggestions---none correct. "A newspaper" he explained. Daddy told jokes, but Mama offered sound advice: "God gave you a gift of 86,400 seconds today. Have you used one to say, "Thank You"?

DAVID, DADDY'S BROTHER

David was a beautiful baby, full of life and his big brother, Jacob loved him! As young as 6 months, laying in his bed, when Jacob walked up to him, and started talking to him, David would get so excited, kicking his legs, swinging his arms, and trying his best to talk with his hero. Jacob would lift him from his bed, walk him from room to room, even outside when the weather was agreeable. Jacob was spoon feed his baby brother and as David grew, Jacob would hold his hands to prevent him from falling as he took his first steps. As David learned to walk, Jacob played with him every day, riding David on his back, lifting him high in the air, and chasing David around the room. By the time David was 2 years old; he would see Jacob walking toward the door and run to meet him. Jacob would scoop him up, hold him close, as they tightly helped each other.

Jacob, a teenager, finally felt truly loved. David woke up early one morning in June, crying fretfully. He had a fever, but his hands and feet were ice cold. He took a sip of milk that he quickly vomited up. His skin was pale and blotchy with rash. He had diarrhea. As the day progressed, he was rapidly deteriorating, his crying just a weak whimper.

Then his body started convulsions, then seizures, and David passed away within a few hours. David had Meningitis, a fungal infection of the lining of the brain and spinal cord. It's caused by a viral infection when bacteria enter the bloodstream and magnifies rapidly releasing toxins that poison the blood. Jacob held his little brother all night, unable to give him up. Why? Why? Dear Lord, why? Jacob silently mourned. The entire family was devastated. Jacob, very seldom mentioned his David to us, but when he did, tears would fill his eyes, the pain still there, still sharp, and deep.

Jesus Christ

Was born in the meanest of circumstances, but the air above was filled with the hallelujahs of the Heavenly hosts. His lodging was a cattle pen, but a star drew distinguished visitants from afar to do Him homage.

His birth was contrary to the laws of life. His death was contrary to the laws of death. No miracle is so inexplicable as His life and teaching.

He had no cornfields or fisheries, but He could spread a table for 5,000 and have bread and fish to spare. He walked on no beautiful carpets, but He walked on the waters, and they supported Him.

His crucifixion was the crime of crimes, but on God's side, no lower price than His infinite agony could have made possible our redemption, When He died few men mourned, but a black crepe was hung over the sun. Though men tremble not for their sins, the earth beneath shook under the load. All nature honored Him; sinners alone rejected Him.

Sin never touched Him. Corruption could not get hold of His body. The soil that had been reddened with His blood could not claim His dust.

Three years He preached His gospel. He wrote no book, built no church, had no money back of Him. After 2,000 years, He is the central character of human history, the perpetual theme of all preaching, the pivot around which the events of the age revolve, the only regenerator of the human race.

Was it merely the son of Joseph and Mary who crossed the world's horizon 2,000 years ago? Was it merely human blood that was spilt on Calvary's hill for the redemption of sinners and which has worked such wonders in men and nations through the centuries?

What thinking man can keep from exclaiming: "MY LORD AND MY GOD!"

Keith L. Brooks

1944

When Daddy fell from the wagon and broke his left elbow into two separate pieces, Dr. Britt had told Daddy that his arm would be permanently stiff, and sure enough, when the cast was finally removed, Daddy's arm was completely stiff, his hand frozen around his neck.

Dr. Britt said, "Your arm might, in time, loosen up some if you can stand the pain of gently moving your arm."

"Nerina, we have a job ahead of us," Daddy informed me when he returned from Dr. Britt's office. "I want you to help me straighten my arm. From now on, every day, I want you to pull on my arm, and I don't care how long it takes or how badly it hurts, we're going to keep at it until I can straighten my arm out."

Daddy sat in a straight back, wooden dining chair with me standing, facing him. I placed my hands around his wrist. Daddy clenched his teeth together and braced himself for the pain.

I pulled Daddy's hand toward me with all my strength. There was absolutely no movement of his arm, and the pain was so excruciating, he could only stand it for an instant. I eased up. I pulled again. I eased up. I pulled again. Again, and again.

Daddy and I continued this therapy, usually three or four times a day. The process was miniscule, the pain agonizing, but the elbow slowly started giving a tiny fraction each week, until finally, Daddy was able to get his hand from his neck, down to his waist, but the elbow was still locked. Next, began the second phase of Daddy's therapy. Lying across the bed on his stomach, his elbow stuck straight up in the air above his back. I would gently push down on the elbow. The pain was tortuous, the progress extremely slow, but after weeks of this daily ritual, Daddy's elbow began to loosen up. Daddy's arm began to straighten out gradually.

Several times a day, every day, Daddy would work his arm up and down, back and forth, from his face to his back until after many weeks, a full range of motion was restored to his arm.

Daddy's depression deepened. The peach crop was either destroyed by a killer frost, making no peaches available to sell, or there was a bumper crop and the markets in the area were flooded with local grown peaches, and Daddy was not able to sell hardly any peaches due to this over abundance.

ORCHARD

The orchard had taken everything the family had to give. From Mama, it had taken nearly all the money she earned at the mill, leaving hardly any money to buy the simple things the family needed. It broke her heart to see her daughters doing without, and that she could not provide better for them.

From Daddy, all his hard work, all his sweat, his worries, his injuries, sometimes even his tears because the sacrifices were having on Mama and the girls, and the uncertainty of his endeavor to produce an income from the orchard.

From the girls, the orchard took new shoes, new clothes, new toys, even food from the table. Additionally, on Saturdays, the older daughters had to help pick up rocks from the fields, load them into the wagon, help hoe the cornfields, plus help their mother with the housework every day after school. They helped gather wood for the cookstove and heaters. If one should become sick, they simply had to "tough it out". There was no going to a dentist or a doctor. Castor oil and Black Draught were their only medications.

- *Inside one of the many rows of peach trees. The entire place was so beautiful when all 22 acres were in bloom.*

The summer of '44 was dry. Mama and Daddy were very concerned that the drought of the 30's had returned. Unlike their first home, located off McKinney Road in Toast, near the Lovill river, this home was not located near a creek or even a branch of water. Irrigation was impossible. The garden just sat there unable to grow and produce. Mama was able to can only 30 ½ gallon jars of green beans, a fraction of the food needed to feed the family the coming winter.

Pinto beans and cornbread, or potatoes and cornbread were our complete meals for the vast majority of those days. During this time, the milk and the milk products prepared by Mama were appreciated even more than ever, if that was possible.

"Mama," I whined. "I get so tired of pinto beans all the time. It sure would be nice to have hamburgers and hot dogs and potato chips and ice cream EVERY day, instead!"

"Honey," Mama answered. "Pinto beans, in fact, all beans are the most nutritious food God gave us to eat. They're full of proteins, plus they also contain potassium, magnesium, folate, iron and zinc, Dr. Britt told me. They are rich in fiber, which helps to keep us regular. Fiber also helps to protect against heart disease, high cholesterol, high blood pressure, and digestive issues, he also said.

"We know that in the Garden of Eden, Adam and Eve had nuts, seeds, fruits and vegetables to gather and eat. These foods were eaten by all the people, and they lived long, healthy lives. Noah lived 950 years, without ever eating burgers, or sugars or salt or ice cream.

"Now, I don't want to live that long, but I do want to live well enough to keep my work done and to have energy to meet my family's needs. I also want to stay slim my entire life and I've found dried beans—all varieties— are full of fiber and slow to digest which keeps me from overeating as Dr. Britt said they would.

"Let's enjoy and appreciate the foods our Heavenly Father made for us," Mama explained. "OK?"

Standing on the back porch each night before bedtime, Mama would watch the huge clouds in the eastern atmosphere. Hundreds of bolts of lightning flashed across the dark sky. The clouds were so far above and away, the sound of thunder could not reach us. As the flashes continued their spectacular display, Mama would say, "These are just electrical storms. No rain in them for us. Maybe, somewhere, it is raining for somebody. I sure hope so. I am sure they need the rain, too."

With Mama at work every day, Daddy tormented with both physical and emotional pains, and my older sisters busy with their own interests and activities, none of them had time for me. I was free to go my own way, to entertain myself, just as long as I stayed in the yard, or in the edge of the woods just beyond the yard.

Oh, how I loved to build playhouses in the very edge of the woods. First, I "borrowed" Daddy's rake and removed all the dead leaves, giving me a clean floor. Next, I brought rocks from the woods and placed them to outline a living room, kitchen, bedroom, and a long driveway. I gathered scraps of boards and short planks from around the barn to make a bed, and a table, a stove, and cupboard in the kitchen. The cupboard shelves were held apart by bricks I borrowed from behind the house. With scraps from old, discarded clothing Mama gave me, I cut a tablecloth, bedcovers, even hung curtains from sticks, then placed them near the outside walls of my playhouse.

From the driveway, I gathered a small container of sand and stirred in just enough water to hold it together. This I packed into two old used canning lids Mama had given me, to form cornbread and cakes. I gathered tiny pebbles from the driveway which were my pinto beans and tore leaves into tiny pieces for a bowl of "greens". Boy, we ate well at my place!

Yes, the playhouse was entertaining, but after two or three hours, I became bored, and was ready for another activity. I played jump rope, hopscotch, and with the kittens and the baby chickens. I walked my doll up and down the driveway, nearly every day, pretending we were visiting friends or buying groceries for our playhouse. I would slide down the cellar door. This was a joyous game, to see how fast I could run up the doors, to quickly set down and slide rapidly down to the ground, and hurriedly continue up and down, up and down, over and over, until most of my flour sack panties Mama made me were worn nearly thread-bare and required patching.

I would set on the front porch swing and sing loudly, "Jesus Loves Me" and "Playmate" until my throat became so dry, I had to go to the kitchen for a drink of water to quench it.

Two Childhood songs

Playmate

O, playmate
Won't you come 'or
And play with me
And bring your dollies three
Climb up my apple tree
Look down my rain barrel
Slide down my cellar door
And we'll be jolly friends forever more.

O, playmate
I can't come 'or
And play with you
My dolly's got the flu

Boo hoo hoo hoo
Can't look down your rain barrel
Or slide down your cellar door
But we'll be jolly friends forevermore.

Jesus Loves Me

Jesus loves me this I know
For the Bible tells me so
To little ones He belongs
They are weak but He is strong
Yes, Jesus loves me, yes Jesus loves me, yes Jesus loves
me
For the Bible tells me so.

Picking Cherries

When the cherries on the tree in the backyard started ripening, the birds swarmed in to devour them. I rushed to the tree in competition with them for the cherries. "These are my cherries, and you can NOT have all of them." I loudly told the birds as I approached the tree to frighten them away.

First, standing on the ground, with a small gallon bucket tied to my waist, I pulled the
lower limbs down and picked all I could reach. Next, I stood on a wooden peach basket and
repeated pulling limbs and picking. Finally, I climbed the tree where I could still pull the limbs
within my reach and picked.

119

The cherries were sour, so I did not eat any as I picked not even one, so I had the bucket filled in an hour or so. I carried the bucket to the kitchen, dumped the cherries into a large pot, drank a glass of water, then returned to the cherry tree. I would pick 2 or 3 times each day until only the very tip-top of the limbs contained cherries I could not reach and these I allowed the birds to have.

After supper, with Mama home from work, and my sisters from school, the family gathered to remove the pits. Mama made pies and later canned all the rest for winter pies. Oh, boy, how the entire family enjoyed those delicious pies!

DADDY

The short, dark days of winter always produced feelings of despondency and acute fatigue for Daddy. Daddy would often state, "I'm so melancholy, I'm not fit to live." Daddy knew he had to fight this feeling with everything he had in him. So early spring was "Tonic" time at our house.

Daddy's first tonic was: SSS Tonic, a brown liquid in a 20 oz. brown bottle. Daddy purchased from Lamb's Drug Store in Mount Airy. One Tablespoon dose once a day at mealtime, provided a therapeutic dosage of Iron, B Vitamins, and other ingredients.

Second Tonic: Asphidity. Asphidity is the sap from the Giant Fennel plant. When grown, slits were cut in the stem of the plant, the sap was drained, collected, and dried. The syrup dried into a soft, lumpy, brown,gummy substance that stunk worse than a dead skunk! It was often called "Devil's Dung". None of us girls could hardly be in the same room with Daddy when he was wearing a small pouch of the stuff around his neck! Daddy vowed he always felt better after these spring tonics. In fact, he was like himself –full of spunk, activities, jokes, singing, and plans for the coming year.

Daddy would work long hours each day, and as warmer weather arrived, many days, he worked so rapidly, his shirt, even the thread holding the buttons onto his shirt, were soaked, completely wet with his perspiration.

1945

Blessings of all blessings on March 4, 1945, Mama gave Daddy a big, beautiful baby boy! After four daughters, Daddy finally had the boy he had always wanted.

- *Our family's pride and joy, Jacob Jr.*

All four of us girls breathed a sigh of relief, now Daddy would not have to trade all four of us for just one boy, as he often teased us, he would, "When he found someone willing to make the trade." Mama gave birth in her bedroom, while us four girls waited quietly and anxiously across the hall in the living room. My sister, Iona, played the phonograph over and over until finally tired from the cranking each record required, she sat down, with her sisters, to wait quietly for the birth, two doors over.

Dr. Britt had arrived to assist in the delivery, and all through the long afternoon, we never heard the doctor or Mama make a single sound. Finally, nearing dark, Dr. Britt, opened the living room door. He immediately fell to the floor and did a rapid summersault across the floor, and then to our open mouth amazement, he turned quickly and did another summersault back across the floor!

"We got a boy!" he exclaimed joyfully, "A big, healthy ten-pound boy, that's what," He laughed and clapped his hands, knowing how badly a boy was wanted.

We girls joined in the laughter, glad our waiting was over, that we could leave the confines of the living room, go see the new baby and Mama, get a drink of water, and eat supper. Boy, I was HUNGRY!

AUBREY

Jacob's younger brother, Aubrey, had received a draft notice shortly after the Japanese bombed Pearl Harbor. The notice did not catch Aubrey by surprise for many young men in the area had received notices during the past twelve months and Aubrey listened to the evening news each day on WPAQ and read both the once- a -week newspapers, Mount Airy News and The Mount Airy Times. He had learned that the German forces were invading their neighboring countries, killing thousands, and that Roosevelt was considering entering the war against Germany.

Aubrey had learned to shoot guns starting at the tender age of 13. He had hunted the woods and fields surrounding his home, for rabbits, squirrels and especially quail that flew over and landed in the hay fields to help provide meat for his family. He had enjoyed working with his rifle and became more serious about his craftsmanship upon hearing the news about the war each evening.

Aubrey reported to Fort Bragg, NC Training Camp for training. There, his sergeant instantly recognized by his gunnery skill. Aubrey could thoroughly clean, load, aim, fire, and hit his targets more accurately and professionally than any recruit his sergeant had encountered before, and to the amazement of all the other recruits watching. Aubrey's sergeant asked him to help his fellow recruits in learning the skill of shooting and the care of his weapons.

After a short furlough to visit his family, and to tell them, "Goodbye" Aubrey, then joined his platoon at Camp Edwards, Massachusetts for further training and from there he was sent to Australia, then to New Caledonia, a French Island, off the coast of Australia.

- *Daddy's brother Aubrey spent all four years in Europe during World War II.*

- *A quoted prayer that Aubrey and his fellow soldiers would say was:*

"I arise today, through God's strength to pilot me,
God's might to hold me,
God's wisdom to guide me,
God's eye to look before me,
God's ear to hear me,
God's word to speak to me,
God's hand to guard me,
God's shield to protect me...."

When Aubrey's daddy did not receive a letter from Aubrey for several weeks, he wrote to Aubrey's commanding officer for news of his well-being. Four long, anxious months later, he received a letter from 1st Lieutenant, Van G. Hartwell, in New Caledonia, stating: (in part) "I assure you that your son, Aubrey is in the best of health and is considered by me to be an ideal soldier. He performs his duties in a very efficient and cheerful manner and is well liked by all the members of the battery. Due to little time to write letters, and seldom chance to mail them once they're written, is the reason his letters are slow in reaching you."

From New Caledonia, Aubrey's unit was shipped to the Salomon's Island. The Japanese wanted and needed the Islands as refueling and supply stations for their troops on their way to invading Australia. The Japanese had nearly irradicated the islands of their inhabitants on the islands leaving dead, decaying bodies of the natives everywhere, lying in piles covered with insects.

There Aubrey's company experienced some of the fiercest fighting of WWII. The island was a military hellhole where the allies and the Japanese Imperial Forces clashed in a brutal struggle for dominance of the islands. The Japanese bombs had left holes in the ground everywhere on the islands, and with the frequent, heavy Pacific rains, all the holes were full of stagnate water. The decaying bodies and the stagnate waters were the perfect breeding environment for mosquitoes. The process for the mosquitoes to reach adulthood, took around twelve days. In the right conditions, mosquito numbers could rise dramatically in only one month. The island was ALIVE with biting insects, ants, and mosquitoes. It was almost impossible for a soldier to speak without an insect flying into his mouth! All the soldiers were instructed to put netting around sleeping and eating areas, to spray the insecticide: DDT, on their clothes, their sleeping areas, into the water holes, on the ground, EVERYWHERE! And to use the spray EVERY DAY!

After many days of battle and the last thirty-six hours of standing guard, Aubrey suddenly became very ill. Aubrey began vomiting, had chills, low blood pressure, and temperature of 106! He had MALARIA!

Many of the soldiers had malaria by this time. Malaria is an illness caused by the Plasmodium parasite. Most often, the female Anopheles mosquito transfers the disease. The parasite enters the blood stream following a mosquito bite. (There are more than one hundred types of Plasmodium, but only five types infect humans. The severity of the illness varies depending on which Plasmodium parasite causes the infection).

First, the parasite multiplies in the human liver, then enters and destroys red blood cells. Symptoms are like a severe flu, but malaria can be long term and fatal.

Quinine was the only medication available to treat malaria. It could NOT cure the disease, only mask the effects of the disease. Quinine was derived from the bark of the cinchona tree that grew in Dutch East Indies.

However, the supply of quinine was all but cut off because the Japanese had invaded the Dutch East Indies and now controlled everything there. This forced the Allies to find and/or develop their own anti-malarial drugs. One was named: Quinacrine, brand name: Atabrine – which while somewhat effective, Atabrine had several side effects, including a tendency to turn a soldier's skin and the whites of his eyes a bright yellow!

The soldiers and their service personnel worked to bury the dead natives, they constantly sprayed DDT and drained stagnate water holes. Malaria became so rapid, with one fourth of the troops on the Pacific Islands infected, resulting in five hundred thousand sick and sixty thousand deaths! A soldier could come down with the disease as much as four different times through the course of one year!

Lieutenant, General Robert L. Eichelbergen, commander of the U. S. Forces bogged down at Buna, "the disease was a sure and more deadly pearl to us than the enemy's marksmanship. We had to whoop the Japanese before the malaria mosquito whipped us!"

After many weeks of fierce fighting with little food or rest, Aubrey was totally exhausted, completely drained both physically and emotionally. When his lieutenant asked him to stand guard duty, Aubrey complied. But it was 36 HOURS LATER before anyone came to relieve him. By this time, Aubrey was so weak, he barely made it to his cot. Aubrey began vomiting, had chills, low blood pressure, and a temperature of 106 degrees. Aubrey had the dreaded MALARIA!

Aubrey was given the new anti-malaria medication: Atabrine, but it came with a bevy of unpleasant, even terrifying side effects, but the medicine did enable Aubrey to leave his cot. The cot was handmade with scrubbed tree branches for the frame and ropes crossed back and forth into squares for the mattress. Dozens of these handmade cots were placed on the bare ground under a tent and there were dozens of these tents on the island where American soldiers were stationed.

Before Aubrey could recover his full strength, however, malaria returned, knocking him flat onto his back once again.

"Malaria is MORE dangerous than enemies' bullets," a US Commander declared! "And every soldier who battles malaria, should be awarded a Badge of Honor!" he declared often.

Again, Aubrey fought his battle with malaria with everything in him: his heart, his mind, his determination, and by talking to his Heavenly Father, every day, humbly asking Him for the strength to win the battle he was fighting.

Aubrey never fully recovered from the malaria sufficiently to regain his strength. One reason: the food supply was very limited (sometimes bananas found in the surrounding hill sides was the only food for several days!). Also, one of Atabrine's most draining side effects was sleep robbing, devastating nightmares. As soon as Aubrey dozed off to sleep, the nightmares returned with a vengeance. Aubrey was unable to rest, and slowly became weaker until he was severely unable to function.

So, when Aubrey's malaria returned for the third time within thirteen months, Aubrey's commander had him airlifted to the hospital in Riverwood, New South Wales, the largest U.S. Military hospital in Australia. The hospital specialized in battle wounds and malaria. Aubrey spent two months recovering in the hospital.

The Australians were aware of the conditions the U.S. Soldiers were enduring, and surviving under, and the people were as involved in the welfare of the U.S. Servicemen, as they were with their own troops. Many Australian families opened their homes and hearts to recuperating war heroes, (as they were considered by the Australians) Aubrey spent 6 months with a family, as he slowly regained his weight, his strength, and his engaging personality. "To know Aubrey was to love him." Everyone who met Aubrey would proclaim.

With the war still raging in Europe, Aubrey was sent to Germany. The allies were slowly advancing east of the German Army and Russian soldiers coming strong west of them. Aubrey was in some of the fiercest battles of the entire war. There was suffering and death everywhere, including the allies, the German soldiers. And the local citizens. To maintain their steady push forward, The American Foot Soldiers needed three items each day, 1. Bullets, 2. Food and rest and, 3. Time to care for their feet. "Trench Foot" is a type of foot damage due to immersion into water and mud and wearing the resulting wet socks and shoes for extended periods of time. This condition caused blisters, blotchy skin, redness, pain, and skin tissue to die and peel off. Prolonged wet feet result in loss of circulation and nerve function, for the skin is derived of oxygen and nutrients the blood normally provides. This can result in the inability to walk and even can lead to gangrene if not treated in time. The condition was rampant among the soldiers due to the heavy rain and melting snow which left the ground wet everywhere.

- *U.S. Soldiers on a snow-covered road in Belgium 1945.*

The treatment for Trench Foot was keeping the feet clean and dry to avoid the infection from starting, and to keep under control once started. Wet feet had to be washed and then thoroughly dried right away once wet, then both dry socks and boots to replace the wet ones. With foot soldiers, that was easier said than done! The supply trucks were following behind, but most days, the trucks were only able to reach the soldiers once a day if that much. Resulting in the soldiers having wet boots and feet nearly every day for long periods.

Many soldiers were sent back to the army doctor's tents stationed behind the battles. Most soldiers recovered and returned to the battlefield within a few days, but a number of soldiers required hospitalization. Aubrey was one of them, but once his feet were mostly healed, he was sent back to the front. The US Army needed EVERY soldier they had for the front lines.

The Germans needed and used the incarnation of people in their concentration camps for a labor supply. The camps were brutal, no food, no water, no warm clothing, little rest on crowded beds, and contagious diseases were rampant. The Germans used gas chambers to "weed out" prisoners who were no longer able to work, and this included not only men, but women and children. Our soldiers had noticed the death odor in the air long before they reached the camp. The German guards had fled the camp before the Allies reached it, in order to save their lives, so many Jewish bodies were left decaying on the ground and in the shelters.

Aubrey had learned of the camps, but was not prepared for the sight awaiting him and his company. When they liberated, Buchenwald on April 11, 1945. Emaciated prisoners were nothing but skin and bones, nearly naked, with haggard faces. They barely looked human!

The weakened prisoners, attempted to thank their liberators, to shake their hands, to give them a hug, but most of them were too weak to stand. They could not even cry, they were so dehydrated.

The army began to feed the soldiers. The soldiers reached for the food greedily and quickly swallowed it without chewing then grabbed for more. Several minutes of this, Lieutenant realized the prisoners were eating too much too fast. After such a long period of starvation, and now, too much food, too quickly, could kill the prisoners just as easily. The food was withdrawn and rationed to them, however, many of the prisoners continued to die for days after their liberation despite the army's medical care, food, and warm clothing, and environmental improvement. The prisoners were just too near death to survive.

The soldiers had noticed the death odor in the air, long before they reached the camp. The German army had fled the camp before the allies reached it, to save their own lives, so many bodies were left decaying on the ground and in the shelters.

As the army began moving the bodies, more and more were found in shallow graves both inside and outside the camp. Aubrey thought he had already seen and experienced everything the war had to show him, but this was far, far, the worst yet. He sincerely doubted the smell of
the decaying bodies would ever leave his nose or spirit.

Hitler committed suicide in May 1945, and the war was winding down. Aubrey was ready to go home. Aubrey had served nearly four years and had earned an Army score of 85 points, which was necessary for an honorable discharge from the army.

His comrades shook his hand, wished him well, and truly admired his character, and his service. Several soldiers told him he was one of the bravest men they'd met, to whom Aubrey would reply, "No, I'm not brave, but I'm in the company of brave men, and it's been richly rewarding to get to know you and serve with you."

Aubrey returned home with several medals and ribbons, which he placed in a box and stored in his attic at home. He didn't want to think about the experiences he had endured to win the medals, but at the same time, he didn't want to throw them away either. Someday—maybe—he might want to see them again, but for the current time, the war was still raging in his head/soul. It would require a LONG time, if ever, before the war was totally over for him.

The reason Aubrey was loved by everyone who knew him was because Aubrey followed Jesus Christ's footsteps and the example Jesus had set forth: The Great Jehovah, Our Heavenly Father was first in Aubrey's heart/soul. His fellowman took second place, and lastly, he, himself, took third place. Aubrey was a TRUE MAN of GOD!

ELECTRICITY

In addition to the one and only son, Jacob Jr. being born and his beloved brother, Aubrey's return home with no life-threatening injuries from his four years of service, the family was blessed with another remarkable blessing. Electricity! Electricity had come to Mount Airy in 1926 and then to the surrounding areas by 1934. It had also been provided to Stuart, Virginia and nearly all the Patrick County, the only area without power was the tiny southwestern tip of Patrick County where we lived.

The main reason for that was because Chunk Harris, the owner of the land west and south of us, would not give the Appalachian Power Company free access to his land to clear a strip of his woods for the power lines to go through from his place to our home and several nearby neighbors.

Harris had allowed the power company access through his woods on the west side of his property to bring electricity to his house, and he despised the strip of cut trees. It made the woods look butchered! No more. No more, he vowed, will another strip be cut through my woods!

When Daddy learned Appalachian Power Company was ready to bring electricity to our home and the six other families, he decided to brave a visit to the Harris home. Harris did not have a friendly or inviting reputation with anyone. He did not attend church or visit anyone, and his only visitors were his two adult sons and their families. So, Daddy was dreading the outcome of his visit.

When Daddy and I arrived at the Harris home, his three big, nasty looking hounds met us on the front porch and instantly gave me a hard time as Daddy knocked, then knocked louder, and continued to knock a third, fourth, even fifth time before Chuck finally answered his door.

The entire time Daddy had knocked on the door and as Daddy and Chuck talked together about getting electricity to his family and the other neighbors, I never understood a word the two men said to each other, because of the dogs. They constantly sniffed my feet, my legs, my back and front, the back of my hair, and they even tried to lick my face with their drooling tongues! I turned around and around as I slapped at them, but I guess they thought I was playing with them, for they continued tormenting me.

Finally, Daddy got his answer, a good one at that, and the dogs, tired from tormenting me, laid back down on the porch.

Daddy and I left the yard. Daddy happy with his success in getting Chuck's permission to cross his land, and me even more, from getting away from those pesky pets. Boy, how I hated big, sloppy mouth dogs!

When our home was wired for electricity, it seemed too good to be true. A whole new world had opened for us! No more buying blocks of ice each summer for the ice box on our back porch to keep the milk, butter, eggs, and cooked foods cold.

With an electric pump at the well, no more winding buckets and buckets of water on laundry days.

- No more winding buckets and buckets of water for the horse drawn sprayer each spring and early summer to spray insecticides on the orchard.
- No more winding buckets and buckets of water for household cleaning, cooking, canning, bathing and drinking.
- No more winding buckets and buckets of water all winter for the cows and horses stationed in the barn.
- No more sitting close to the kerosene lamps for light to see to read, write, or sew.

- No more sitting by the static filled battery radio trying to understand the daily news.
- No more carrying the kerosene lantern during the cold short days of winter to the barn to milk the cows and still hardly seeing the ground in front of our feet.
- No more winding buckets and buckets of water for the family's Saturday night baths in the zinc tub
- No more stumbling around in a dark room. For now, the room could be flooded with light at the mere pull of a string hanging from the center of the ceiling!

Oh, the wonder of it all!

The past three years, Mama had worked to pay in full several small debts, and plus the bigger debt owed to the Farmers Home Administration in Stuart. So, once again, Mr. P. H. Bowman allowed Daddy and Mama to borrow money, this time for the well pump, and to have a "modern kitchen" installed.

Twelve feet of wooden cabinets were built along the outside wall of the kitchen, with a double sink, double windows over the sink, and quarter shelves on each side. Mama decorated the shelves with ceramic roosters and hens and planted "wandering dew" in each one.

Next, a dining nook was built on the easy end of the room, with windows on two sides to let in plenty of sunlight. The walls were painted a dark green and linoleum flooring of several shades of yellow was placed on the floor.

The room was furnished with a 22.6 cubic foot Frigidaire Refrigerator and a Maytag wringer washing machine. A brand new bright red Philco electric radio was placed on the counter next to the outlet. Boy, the room was so fresh and modern!

Mama said, "I don't want an electric stove. I do not know how to work it. I might burn the bread, or worse yet,

I might let a pot catch on fire and burn the house down! Besides, we need the wood burning stove to warm the kitchen in cold weather." she reasoned. So, Mama did not get an electric stove as most of our neighbors did.

But Mama was ecstatic! Water! Water for the first time in her life, was at the mere turn of a faucet and lights at the pull of a string! What more could a person ask for!

Mama did not return to the mill after the birth of her son, Jacob Jr. Mama told me the reason for this was she wanted to be a full-time mother to her infant son, and to also be with me as she had worked in the mill my entire life, leaving me five days a week for the mill, and she wanted to spend time with me before I started school.

Mama told my sister, Audrey, the reason she did not go back to work was her painful feet. After standing in one place for eight years in cheap, thin shoes that gave her feet no support, the bottoms of her feet were covered in calluses and corns, making standing painful. Her feet needed a rest.

Mama told Daddy she was leaving her job because she needed to be at home with their son, to help with raising a larger garden to feed their family, and because her feet hurt painfully when standing. But the most important reason she left was due to the fact she could no longer put her money into a losing orchard. She knew Daddy had put his heart and soul into the orchard and had a beautiful place to show for it, and that it was not his fault that the market for peaches were completely flooded each year. Too many peaches were brought in from Georgia, North and South Carolina, plus the numerous orchards near our southwestern Virginia home.

Daddy stepped outside and, on his knees, "Thank you, Heavenly Father, for my wife's safe delivery and the birth of a healthy son."

The spring was unseasonably warm, in fact the entire winter had been warmer than usual, and the orchard was covered in tiny pink buds. Another week to ten days of the warm weather and the entire orchard would be in full bloom.

April 12th, as had taken place before, a nor'easter was on its way. Once again, Daddy did everything he could possibly do to save the tiny peach inside each blossom, but again to no avail. The peaches had been killed by the freeze.

All spring and summer, Daddy marveled at God's Goodness in giving him a precious family and new son, his brother's safe return from the war, and the marvel of electricity in his home, but he was very concerned as to how he would provide for his family for the long months ahead, even how he would pay the new monthly electric bill.

It seemed to Daddy that life was a constant mixture of good and bad, right or wrong, dark or light. It seemed when God lifted him up onto a mountain high, the Devil came along and knocked him down. Or, when in a dark pit spiritually, then God lifted him up again, and revealed His Love, Grace, and Mercy to him.

CHECKERS

Daddy often visited Robert Green for a game of checkers, whenever the weather or the crops would allow each man a little free time. They both took the game seriously, and each gave the game their undivided attention and concentration. Despite Dad giving the game everything, he had, Robert won six out of every ten games they played.

One September, Saturday evening, Daddy took the well-worn path through the woods to Robert's place. The "short cut" was still a mile or more, but was "straight as the crow flies", to Robert's tobacco barn.

- By 9 P.M, and bedtime, Daddy had not returned home. Mama became concerned and worried. Where was Jacob?
- By 11 P.M., Mama could not lie in bed another moment. Something had happened to Daddy.
- By 1 A.M., Mama was praying and walking the floor. She even stepped out into the yard and called his name several times. Daddy could be lying in the woods, hurt, or with a broken leg, or worse.
- By 3 A.M., Mama was nearly hysterical, her prayers more insistent. Daddy had NEVER spent the night away before and Mama knew, just knew, something awful had happened to Daddy for him to be gone all night!
- By 5 A.M., Sick with worry and grievously distressed, Mama prayed humbly, beseeching the Almighty to please grant Daddy a safe return home.

"Dear Father, you know the kids and I cannot survive without him." She wept.

- By 7 A.M., Daddy stepped out of the woods, tired, but okay.

Mama ran to him, to inquire if he was hurt, or what had happened to him, and why had he been gone all night?

"Why, I told you I was going to Robert's to play a game of checkers. He was firing a barn of tobacco, so I sat with him at the barn and the next thing I knew, the sun was coming up! I didn't plan to stay so long, but I was so interested in the game, that time just slipped away from us." Daddy told Mama," You shouldn't have worried about me. I was just with Rob playing checkers."

The men's night of fun and checkers had cost Mama a night of peace and rest.

I Wish I Was a Single Girl Again

(Irish Song)

When I was single, I went dressed up so fine
Now I am married, Lord I go ragged all the time
Oh, Lord, don't I wish I was a single girl again
I got dishes to wash and springs to go to
When you are married, Lord, you know you got it all to do
Oh, Lord, I wish I was a single girl again
Yeah, oh Lord, don't I wish I was a single girl again
Yeah, oh Lord, don't I wish I was a single girl again.

Yes, Daddy had spent the entire night playing
checkers with Robert. Concentrating on the
game and trying to win was a slight diversion from
worrying about his financial situation and
what to do about it. What should he do? What could he do?
Daddy could see NO answer. NO hope. Anywhere.
Anymore. Just ROT! ROT! ROT!

1945 had been a mixture of joy and sorrow,
happiness and worry, laughter and tears, times of
desperately pleading with God for His Mercy, to times of

praising God for all His Blessings bestowed each day upon the family.

"God will provide", Mama assured Daddy. "We'll make it somehow, at least we are all well, and that's the main thing. Not having any money is an inconvenience, but that is all it is, just an inconvenience. Remember, when we think of all the things we do not have, we make ourselves poor; when we count all the blessings we do have, then we are rich. Truly rich!"

1946

Uncle Audrey had returned home. He looked wonderful and had received big "WELCOME HOME" hugs from his sisters and sister-in-law. Strong handshakes from his dad, brothers, and brothers-in-law. Audrey came home with a large box of Hershey candy bars. He gave a bar to each of his nieces and nephews and received big welcome home hugs and kisses in return.

As with most battle-weary veterans, the war comes home with them.

- Aubrey could be outside in the bright sunshine fully occupied by his activity, when suddenly, planes were flying overhead, dropping bombs, blowing buildings, homes, even the soldiers running pass him to oblivion.

- When driving along a highway with large trees, beside the road ahead, a sudden "caution" gripped him—both German and Japanese had hidden in trees waiting to ambush the advancing soldiers. Soldiers were shot, some killed, before their hiding place was located and fire returned.

- A low rumble of distant thunder was an armored tank division coming toward him with total annihilation as their object.

- Sound asleep, Aubrey would suddenly awaken and quickly scramble from his bed, seeking cover from Germans shooting at him from the foot of his bed.

-

- Occasionally, when eating and thoroughly enjoying his food, the food on his plate, suddenly changed into the look and smell of dead Jewish prisoners.

141

Repulsed, Aubrey would push his plate away,
unable to eat another bite.

The flashbacks were so real to Aubrey, they caused his heart to race frantically, to sweat profusely, and difficulty in breathing. Aubrey would pitifully whisper Jesus's name. That was all he could do, but Jesus always heard him. Aubrey could feel Jesus's presence, His comfort, and Aubrey's heart would slowly calm down, and his breathing gradually returned to normal. Aubrey never shared his flashbacks with anyone, not even his daddy until much later. Aubrey had Jesus, the One who had been with him all four years of war and Aubrey needed Jesus equally now.
Thank you, Jesus, for the ones who love you, You're both their strength and their Peace.

GARDEN

As Mama and Daddy planted, weeded, and gathered the garden, and Mama canned the vegetables, it was my responsibility to entertain my brother, which was a totally enjoyable chore. I carried him on my left hip part of everyday. I had to "cock" my hip up to give him a place to sit and hold my arms around his waist to keep him secure.
Within a few weeks, my left hip started hurting every afternoon around 2 o'clock. The pain was strong enough that Mama allowed me to lay down to rest. The pain usually lasted about two hours, and then I was ready to resume playing with my brother.
Unfortunately, the pain gradually became more intense during the next three weeks until Daddy, very concerned, took me to Dr. Richards's office. Lying on the exam table, he pointed out to Daddy that my left hip was lower than my right hip, which was the result of carrying

142

my brother on that side. Dr. Richard adjusted my hip back to its proper place and advised Daddy I shouldn't be carrying my brother so much.

Jacob Jr. had boundless energy and was easy to please. All he required was to be kept fed and dry. We played chase, played with the kittens, swung on the front porch swing, even chased the half-grown chickens through the yard. I hurried behind him, trying to keep him from running through the small patches of clover scattered throughout the yard. The blooming clover attracted the bees and if we, barefooted, ran through the patch would get stung every time! Boy, did those beestings hurt! I was almost glad when I learned by stinging me, the bees would die. Serves them right for causing so much pain!

Mama would mix a level teaspoon of baking soda with just enough water to make a paste. Then, apply the paste directly on the sting site, and the pain would slowly and gradually fade away. After the pain was gone, the place was washed, then a spoonful of honey was rubbed on the site to help relieve the itching.

Yes, Jacob Jr., was an extremely busy young fellow, until one Saturday afternoon when he came to a sudden and drastic stop. He started crying and continued to cry as both Mama and Daddy tried to comfort him, but nothing helped, and his crying only grew more inconsolable. Then, Mama saw an unusual bulge below his belly button and instantly knew this was something serious.

Daddy hurried to Milton's store to use the new telephone Milton recently had installed and called Dr. Britt at his home. Daddy explained Jacob Jr.'s symptoms and Dr. Britt agreed Jacob needed to be seen by a doctor immediately.

Dr. Britt wasted no time getting to our home and going straight to the distraught young fellow. He talked

- *Another picture of my little brother, Jacob Jr.*

softly to him as he gently rubbed his belly. Then, Dr. Britt gently and carefully pushed the knot back into its proper spot and the horrible pain was instantly relieved.

Dr. Britt explained that Jacob Jr. had a "rupture". A rupture is caused when a part of the intestine pushes through a weak spot in the belly muscle. Dr. Britt stated,

"These ruptures could happen again at any time. He may require surgery if this happens several times, but usually the place heal on its own. Only time will tell."

The following week, Jacob Jr.'s stomach was very tender. He didn't have an appetite and he was weak and drained. He slept long naps each day. Gradually, he regained his strength and returned to being the playful brother I knew and loved.

In the following two years, Jacob Jr. had three more episodes and Dr. Britt rushed to his aid each time. The weak spot closed at the age of four years, and Jacob Jr. was not troubled another time.

Thank you, Heavenly Father, for healing my brother, and please continue to protect and bless Dr. Britt and Dr. Richards.

SWEET PEA

I LOVED and drank fresh milk three times a day. I LOVED butter on hot biscuits. I LOVED the biscuits and cornbread made with buttermilk.

That is except in early spring. In early spring while all the other greens lay dormant, wild green onions were the first to sprout from the ground, and boy, did Sweet Pea and Molly love the fresh green taste. They ate everyone they could find and searched for more. But the onions totally and destroyed the taste of their milk, butter, and even their buttermilk, making it revolting to smell or taste, and had to be thrown out for no one would drink it. Even the mama cat or a stray dog walking through the yard, wouldn't touch the foul stuff. This horrible taste lasted for five days or longer, until the regular grasses overtook the onions and the cows turned to eating them instead.

Oh, thank goodness this only occurred once a year, and thank goodness it didn't last any longer than it did.

Sweet Pea and Molly, Mama's two Jersey milk cows, were in heat. It had been over a year since their last calving and their milk was slowly but steadily drying up. Cows produce milk to feed their babies, not to feed humans.

Jersey cows are the ladies of the cattle kingdom. They are petite, with small faces and short horns, and possess an easy, mild personality. Their milk is the best tasting, most nutritious, and was easily turned into butter, cheese, and buttermilk which Mama kept ready for cooking and for her table. But they became just ordinary cows when they were in heat, full of rebellion, stubborn, and cantankerous. Daddy could not afford to buy and feed a stud bull for just two milk cows.

The nearest bull was nearly two miles away at the dairy operated by Uncle Herbert. Daddy did not have the heart to ask Uncle Herbert to interrupt his overworked days to come and pick-up Daddy's cows in his truck and carry them to his farm and bull. It would take three or four hours from his busy day and the same amount of time to return the cows. Additionally, Daddy did not want both cows to "calf" at the same time. To keep a constant supply of milk, it was necessary for the cows to "calf" three or four months apart.

Daddy decided to walk Sweet Pea to Uncle Herbert's farm and the stud bull there. Since Sweet Pea had been the one which had been the longest time to have calved so she would be the one to go to Uncle Herbert's dairy. It would be quite a trip for Daddy and Sweet Pea. Over a dirt road, through the woods, through a wide meadow, and across a forty-foot wooden bridge, but Daddy was confident Sweet Pea could easily make the trip. Daddy asked me to come along on this trip to walk behind Sweet Pea as he led her by a short rope tied to her halter. Oh boy, I was ready for the adventure! I loved Sweet Pea. I loved going to Uncle Herbert's. I loved being with Daddy, and it was a perfect fall day for an outing.

Sweet Pea came along amiably, and we made good time walking the road to Uncle Herbert's dairy. Sweet Pea seemed to be enjoying the adventure also. She only stopped occasionally to nibble at clumps of grass along the edge of the road or to do her "business".

That is, until we came to the bridge crossing Lovill's Creek. For some reason known only to her, Sweet Pea stopped at the very edge of the bridge and would not place a hoof on the wooden boards.

Daddy rubbed her back, smoothed her neck softly, talked to her to encourage her to step up on the bridge. She would not. Daddy placed the bucket of feed under her nose to tempt her forward. She took a bite but would not follow the bucket when Daddy moved it forward over the bridge. Daddy kept tempting her with the food. Daddy could have led her through the water to the other side of the creek, but there was a five-strand barbed wire fence on both sides of the bridge. Also, between the water and the fence, was a steep incline covered in overgrowth bushes, trees, and debris that had washed down along the creek during periods of heavy rain.

The only way to the bull waiting at the dairy was to cross the bridge. Daddy patted Sweet Pea's rump. He talked to her. He gave her more feed. He prompted her. He patiently and calmly, kept coaching her to get her to step up on the bridge. She would not budge. Finally, Daddy began to lose his cool. He had tried every trick in the book with no success. He had given her plenty of time. It was now time to stop coddling Sweet Pea and get her across the bridge. Daddy was determined to make it happen. Daddy firmly pulled on Sweet Pea's lead rope. Sweet Pea would not budge. Daddy kept pulling, Sweet Pea maintained her staunch stand. Daddy pulled the rope with all his strength. Sweet Pea advanced a step, but as soon as Daddy eased his pulling to catch his breath, Sweet Pea took two steps backward. Daddy kept trying. Forward - Backward. Forward - Backward. Forward- Backward. "Get a switch and whip her backside." Daddy told me. I did. My taps with the switch went unnoticed. "Switch her harder and faster." Daddy commanded as he continued to pull on the rope with all his might. I did. Sweet Pea ignored us.

Daddy took a few deep breaths. He allowed Sweet Pea to take a break. He gave me a timeout, also. Minutes later, Daddy, more determined than ever, started the struggle with the cow all over again. Sweet Pea stood firm. Daddy was becoming more aggravated by the minute with Sweet Pea. He broke an even longer, keener, switch and gave her a good smack across her rear end. Sweet Pea flinched but did not move forward. "Here, you pull her, and I'll push her," Daddy said. We switched ends. I pulled with all my strength. I was nearly lying flat on the bridge. Daddy pushed with all his determination, his feet kicking up gravel in the road. Sweet Pea's neck was stretched out to the limit, her rear end was hunched up to her front feet, but Sweet Pea remained firmly planted.

By now, Daddy and I had been working with Sweet Pea for over an hour. Trying to nudge, prod, and encourage Sweet Pea to step up on the bridge. She continued to refuse. She was not an inch closer to the edge of the bridge than when we first started.

Daddy was exhausted and totally exasperated with the entire situation. Without thinking, and as almost a reflex action, he hauled off and kicked Sweet Pea on her shin. Sweet Pea jumped. Daddy grabbed his foot with both hands and hobbled around and around. He had knocked his big toe out of joint. Poor Daddy, silently, limped home with the sprained toe. We returned Sweet Pea to the pasture. She was still in heat and still as pig headed and mule stubborn as before her trip, only more so.

In the house, Daddy carefully removed his shoe. Holding his foot steady, he asked Mama to give his big toe a sudden, hard pull. The toe popped back into place and the pain was instantly gone.

The next time Daddy went to Milton's, Daddy told him about the ordeal, knowing Milton would get a big laugh from it. Milton did. He laughed for several minutes, clapped his hands and shook his head.

Then, he told Daddy, "The next time you try this, when you get the cow to the bridge, place your shirt or jacket over her head and face to blind her. I've heard that if a cow can't see the openings in the bridge, she will walk on it."

"Does it really work?" Daddy asked, amazed. The problem could be solved this easily and quickly?

"I'm not sure, I've never tried it, but it's worth a try." Milton replied.

It did work, when Daddy and I walked Sweet Pea to visit Uncle Herbert's bull again.

When Irish Eyes are Smiling

There's a tear in your eye, And I'm wondering why,
For it never should be there at all.
With such pow'r in your smile, Sure a stone you'd beguile,
So there's never a teardrop should fall.
When your sweet lilting laughter's Like some fairy song,
And your eyes twinkle bright as can be;
You should laugh all the while And all the other times
smile,
And now, smile a smile for me.

When Irish eyes are smiling,
Sure, 'tis like the morn in Spring.
In the lilt of Irish laughter
You can hear the angels sing.
When Irish hearts are happy,
All the world seems bright and gay.
And when Irish eyes are smiling,
Sure, they steal your heart away.

For your smile is a part of the love in your heart,
And it makes even sunshine more bright.
Like the linnet's sweet song, Crooning all the day long,
Come your laughter and light.
For the springtime of life Is the sweetest of all
There is ne'er a real care or regret;
And while springtime is ours Throughout all of youth's
hours,
Let us smile each chance we get.

The orchard produced the largest, prettiest, most delicious peaches ever, but it made no difference, only the regular buyers came and nearly the entire crop fell to the ground to rot.

When Daddy stepped outside during the day, there they lay. When lying in his bed in total darkness, all he could hear was their dropping to the ground. The sight and sound was driving him CRAZY! He and Mama had put everything they had into the orchard, and all they got in return was disappointment, debts, and injured bodies!

"Oh, Lord, have mercy."

ROT! ROT! ROT! Throughout each long night, tormented him. The world, everything, was useless and hopeless. ROT! ROT! ROT!

SCHOOL 1946

The first day of school! Oh, how excited I was! Mama had found time somehow, to make five new brightly colored cow-feed sack dresses for me plus, five new "droopy drawers" from white flour sacks. They were called "droopy" because they were kept up with a drawstring, that was pulled tightly and tied at the waist. The fabric was rather stiff, so the string could easily work loose causing the panties to slip and fall to the floor if I wasn't paying attention and held the clumsy loose-legged garments up! Mama had also bought me a pair of shoes! Yes, I am ready for school. After walking to the NC/VA borderline, there stood all the neighborhood kids...the Tolbert and Harris boys, and Linda and Carol Worrell to await with me for the bus. Once the bus arrived, the boys scrambled with each other, to be the first to enter the bus and reach their favorite back seat! Then the sisters, with me last. I struggled up the two steep steps of the bus, to find to my amazement: NOSEATS! Only one long leather-covered bench!

Starting on the right, behind the driver, all the way down the bus, across the back, and all the way up the left side to the front in one solid bench! One solid piece! There was also a bench down the center of the bus with no back or handles anywhere, just slick, smooth, worn, leather. I sat down behind the driver.

- *Nerina (me) age 6, first year in school at North Main St School in Mt. Airy N.C.*

As the bus continued to fill, every time the driver stopped to pick up more students (our stop was the first students to be picked up), the boys in the back would fall forward against, and push the students toward the front of the bus. With the seats worn smooth, the push was easy for them, and nearly every student ended up in a pile at the front of the bus, around the driver, the door, and me.

The driver would fuss at the boys in the back, but being a high school student himself, they paid little attention to him. The boys might slow down for the next stop or two, to soon continue their game. However, the trip home in the afternoon, the boys didn't let up and every stop was an uncontrollable slide of students to the front, and I was getting mashed, as the students piled on me! I was never really hurt, but it was uncomfortable and required time for all the kids to straighten up and return to their seats.

Both the Harris and Tolbert boys were full of mischief, if not downright mean. They often had fights with other boys on the bus and in the back playground after school. The next day would be a trip to the office, where Miss Minick, the principal, would talk to the boys, remind them of the school's rules, threaten to visit and tell their parents, even to expel them from school if their disruptive activities continued. The boys calmed down for a week or so, but their mischief gradually but steadily returned to be repeated.

One morning, with the school bus slowly coming to a stop, one of the Harris boys fell and the front tire of the bus ran over his right leg. He wasn't badly hurt, but a trip to Miss Minick's office earned him a two-week vacation.

On cold winter mornings, the boys often gathered dry corn stalks lying in the field bordering our waiting place and built a fire with them to keep all of us warm. Boy, we appreciated the warmth the fires provided as we waited. especially the numerous mornings, the bus was "broke down" which resulted in a 2 hour wait for another bus to come and pick us up. I never learned what "break down" meant, just that it occurred often and resulted in a long day for all the students on the route. (All of them, however lived close to the hard top road, so they didn't have to battle the weather, as they could wait for the bus inside their homes). This "break down" resulted in a long day for us as we had to wait after school until the other bus made its regular run. The other driver (another teenage boy) would then take us home. I'd be completely pooped by the time I reached home.

- *North Main St School, Mt Airy N.C.*

Besides the fires, the boys (all older than me) yelled at passing cars, causing the drivers to instantly turn their heads and often swerve on the road. They wrestled with each other and threw rocks they gathered from the gravel road where we waited. One morning, in early May, one of their thrown rocks, hit Linda, (who was smiling at her sister) in her mouth, tragically breaking one of her permanent incisors. The blow was so sudden and powerful that the broken piece of tooth flew to the back of Linda's mouth, causing her to swallow it instantly. Linda cried from both pain and fear of what her parents might say to her later that day when they returned home from work. This time the boys received a 3-week vacation, after visiting Miss Minick's office.

The days the boys did attend school, they managed to smuggle 4 cigarettes (one for each of them) and a small book of matches to school nearly every day, to smoke during their lunch break, at the back of the baseball field. This was the worst offense the boys could commit. Any boy caught smoking a cigarette was automatically and permanently expelled. If they wanted to continue their education, they would have to attend a different school!

Linda and Carol no longer rode the bus since the tooth incident. So, on the way home, after being let off the bus, I walked as fast as I could up the road. I wasn't afraid of the boys, because they mostly ignored me, but at the same time, I didn't want to associate with them.

Some days, they would walk fast, and get far ahead of me, sometimes, they lingered slowly up the road far behind me. Occasionally, they threw rocks my way. The rocks always landed far ahead or to my side off the road and I knew they were not aiming at me, only teasing me, to see my reaction. I ignored both them and their rocks.

When I reached my long driveway, I slowed down and leisurely strolled along as the boys continued on the hard top road to their homes further up the road.

The first day of school, Mrs. Poore, my teacher, had trouble pronouncing my name, and called out "The Mosley Girl" and when no one answered, I realized she was calling me. Everything went well for me inside her classroom, but I soon learned the situation was completely different outside, in the hall or on the playground. You see, I was one of the poorest dressed girls in school. The girls asked me where in the world did I get the funny dresses I wore? Why did I wear boys' socks only? Why didn't I bring a dodgeball or a jump rope to play with? The most often asked question: What was wrapped inside the newspaper bundle I brought to school each day?

I didn't take offense concerning my dresses. As to my socks, I explained that my sister, Audrey, was working at Renfro Knitting Mill, and only brightly colored striped boys' socks were made on the floor she worked. She could buy the socks at a reduced price, and that's why I wore boys' socks. The question about my socks makes me conscious of being different. I was the ONLY girl in the entire school wearing boys' socks.

When I explained that I had my lunch inside the newspaper bundle, they laughed, and told others who also laughed. You see, all the other children ate in the delicious smelling lunchroom. A few students packed their lunch and ate in the classroom at their desk. Their banana and bologna-cheese sandwiches were wrapped in wax paper and carried in brown lunch bags. They purchased a carton of milk from the lunchroom to accompany their sandwiches.

I quickly learned it was better to keep my lunch private. When the lunch bell rang, I would grab my package, and join the other girls in the restroom who were washing their hands before eating in the lunchroom.

When the girls left the restroom, I locked myself in a booth and quickly swallowed 2 or 3 bites of the honey biscuit Mama had made that morning. Then I unlocked the door and threw the remaining parts into the trash can. I washed my hands and drank greedily from the nearby water fountain.

Then, I rushed out the door into the empty playground. All the other students were still inside eating their lunches.

I felt a little embarrassed by my being so sneaky, but it didn't compare to the embarrassment I would experience if I ate my newspaper wrapped biscuit without a drink for my lunch in their presence. Just better to eat in privacy and keep my lunch to myself.

Each and every afternoon, when I reached the lower part of my yard, everything was once again fully okay with me. The huge, green yard, Mama's flowers, the lush peach orchard, and the velvet blue mountains greeted my return home. Oh, how I LOVED the beauty and sanctity of the place! I knew the girls at school who laughed at my socks, my dresses, and my newspaper wrapped lunch had NOTHING at their home to compare to the beauty of my home. So, girls, I'm not the poor one---you are!

Once or twice, I told Mama about the girls at school, and how they laughed at me, leading to feelings of inferiority.

Mama would tell me "Nerina, you're paying too much attention to the girls. Remember: When we look downward and inward, we will become very depressed. When we look outward and around us, at others, we'll be disappointed and disillusioned. When we look upward, we are delighted, loved, and complete. Keep your eyes lifted." She sweetly advised me.

1947

Raising a garden was a year-round project. It was a job both Mama and Daddy enjoyed doing, but a job they took very seriously. The garden was the family's food supply. No garden: no food, it was just that simple, just that essential.

All the work necessary to grow a garden was put on a schedule, and the schedule was followed faithfully.

By the end of October, all the vegetables had been harvested and the weeds have completely taken over the garden, so, the garden had to be "cleaned-up" from the previous summer's weeds and mess.

Daddy "hitched" Sadie and Neil to the sickle mower and cut the abundant growth to the ground. Next, the heavy "bog" with its cutting edges, were dragged over the garden numerous times to mix the vegetation in the soil. The vegetation would decay during the coming winter months and help to enrichen the soil.

Next, with the garden dormant and soil resting, it was time to fertilize the land for next year's production, and the very best fertilizer for this job was FREE. It just needed to be moved. The cow manure in the barn from the previous winter had dried during the hot summer months. The dead leaves placed in each stall several times during the winter months to help keep the cow's feet dry had completely decomposed with the manure, and this made a potent fertilizer for the garden.

So, Daddy, one shovel full at a time, loaded the horse drawn wagon to the top of its rim. Next, Daddy "hitched" Sadie and Neil to the wagon, and horses pulled the wagon to the garden. Again, one shovel full at a time, Daddy spread the manure evenly over the garden. Daddy, simply, gave a short whistle and the horses knew to pull up another fifteen feet to stop and wait as Daddy, again, spread the compost around the wagon.

In addition to this fertilizer, Daddy would spread a light covering of limestone over the garden every second or third year to "sweeten" the soil. Every five or six years, the garden was moved to a new area on the farm. This new garden was necessary to allow for crop rotation and also because the manure not only grew vegetables, it grew humongous weeds as well, and these weeds slowly, but steadily "took-over" the garden.

By December 15th, Daddy plowed the soil as deeply as the two horses could pull the plow through the ground. The coming cold weather would freeze the ground and during the winter's warm days, the ground would thaw. This repeated freeze/thaw over the winter resulted in a deep topsoil.

By the first of February, any rocks larger than a plate was picked up, loaded on the wagon, then hauled to the low places in our long driveway and placed in the ruts to help in the constant battle of road repair.

By the first of March, Daddy and the horses dragged the heavy "harrow" back and forth, up and down, again back and forth numerous times through the soil to make the ground completely level and lump free, turning the dirt into soft loam perfect for planting the garden.

Oh, the dirt smelled so good! I loved to smell it. It smelled fresh - new - like spring!

By March 15th, with Sadie pulling the lay-off plow, Daddy meticulously laid off perfectly straight planting rows east to west across the garden and each row was the exact same distance apart. A fine layer of Royster fertilizer was spread into the center of each row, and I dragged the hoe through the fertilizer to mix it with the soil to prevent the fertilizer from "burning" the seeds.

Next, the first garden was planted: turnip greens, kale, and lettuces were sown. Plus, beets, carrots, (Mama-soaked carrot and beet seeds for 24 hours before planting, then rolled the seeds in wood ashes. This made the seeds sprout stronger and the vegetables a better color than without this application.) green peas, and numerous rows of potatoes. Small onion sets were carefully, one at a time, buried ½ their level into the soil. Also, three dozen cabbage plants were "pegged" into the ground.

Mama always saved vegetable seeds from the previous summer's garden in order to have the seeds needed to plant the following year's garden. Squash, cucumber, (Cucumber seeds, Mama learned, age well. Seed from 2 to 4 years old is preferrable to newer seeds. Newer seeds tend to have luxuriant vines, but sprout slower than aged seeds, and are not quite as productive. She never used seeds over 4 years old, as they were found too weakened to produce.) and pumpkin seeds were plentiful and easy to separate from their pulp.

Bean and peas were allowed to hang on their vines until their outer shell was mostly dry, then picked and shelled. The seeds, one variety at a time, was spread out onto boards near the window in the attic to finish drying. It was a tedious job for Mama getting the seeds up and down the ladder to the attic (the small ladder was located against the wall in the bedroom closet), but the attic was the perfect place for drying seeds as it ensured no birds, insects, or chickens could get to the seeds, plus the sun's daily warmth made the seeds dry easily and quickly. The dried seeds were placed into the one-gallon glass jugs coffee had come in, and then the lid was screwed down. The jars were stored in the hall closet for safe keeping.

All "greens" produced abundant flowerheads with hundreds of seeds inside each. These flower heads were stored in large paper bags, then placed in the attic to finish drying.

By March 15th, a small plant bed was sown with tomato and sweet pepper seeds. Mama placed at least 6 whole sweet potatoes into a raised hill covered with rotted sawdust and the potatoes would sprout several plants each to be reset into rows in the May Garden.

The night before planting, the needed number of seeds were placed into small bowls, then covered with lukewarm water to set overnight. This water soaked the seeds outer crust and helped to hasten the seeds' germination.

The seasons the garden produced abundantly, Mama saved extra seeds, to exchange with family and neighbors for seeds she didn't have, plus she often gave seeds to neighbors who needed them. It gave Mama great pleasure to help someone in need.

- *One of my mom's many gardens.*

Mama used the moon signs, given in the Old Farmer's Almanac, to plant the garden. She fully believed planting by the moon made the gardens more productive. Above ground vegetables: corn, beans, etc. were planted by the "light of the moon" - the nights when the moon's surface light was gradually increasing. Below ground vegetables, potatoes, beets, etc. were planted by the "dark of the moon" - when the night's moonlight was gradually decreasing.

In addition to planting by the correct moonlight, Mama also planted by the Zodiac, when it was in the "arms" or "legs" - she was careful to avoid the "head" and "feet" signs. "Companion" planting was important too: onions with beets, carrots with lettuce, potatoes with cabbage, cucumbers with peas, beans with corn. However, she never planted cucumbers with squash in rows side by side; for both would grow large robust vines, with huge blooms, but the blooms resulted in very few vegetables. Very few.

The second and largest garden was planted by May 15th. Numerous rows of green beans, corn, along with squash, cucumber, tomato and pepper plants, sweet potato plants, a dozen hills of watermelon, and six hills each of pumpkin and winter squash, completed the May Garden.

The third garden was planted by July 15th. Again, beans, corn, cucumber, and squash were planted, also a second large patch of potatoes for late fall harvesting.

By August 15th, the fourth garden was a large plot of "greens": turnip, mustard, kale, and lettuces, (The tiny seed of all greens, are too small to be planted alone. They could easily be sewn too thickly, resulting in insufficient room for the roots to grow—especially turnips needed room to grow and reach maturity. Mama always mixed the seeds before planting with fine sand to prevent sowing them too thickly.) Two dozen cabbage plants were also planted. This garden ensured fresh vegetables, until the very coldest of winter nights. Mama often spread a double layer of old cheesecloth (from Daddy's tobacco growing days) over the greens to protect them from freezing, and this continued their availability into the start of the new year or, if the winter was mild, even later.

Planting the garden at separate intervals ensured a steady supply of vegetables, plus enabled Mama to can and preserve the abundance over a longer period.

As soon as the young vegetables in the garden was six inches high, Daddy "hitched" Sadie to the cultivator and together, they carefully loosened the soil between each row, dislodging any young weeds in the space and bringing fresh soil to the surface. This cultivation was done one more time, as the vegetables were growing, to ensure no weeds took hold and smothered out the vegetables in their competition with the weeds, for the sun, rain, and soil nutrients that fed the vegetables, enabling the vegetables to grow robustly.

After Daddy had cultivated the rows, Mama, and I, with hoe in hand, tediously removed any weeds around the growing vegetables. Then, with the hoe, we brought fresh dirt up and around the tender plants, to help preserve moisture and promote root growth.

"Why do weeds have to grow?" I asked Mama as I hoed the ugly things.

"Well, honey, if the soil couldn't grow weeds, then it couldn't grow our vegetables either," Mama replied. "Everything has its advantages and disadvantages. It's up to us which we concentrate on and use to our benefit."

During the second cultivation, a "side-dressing" of nitrate of soda (a spoonful) was dropped at each vegetable plant. Then Daddy, dragged the cultivator along beside the row to incorporate the soda into the soil. The soda caused the vegetables to grow as if they'd been fed steroids or something.

Whee! - for me the job of hoeing the garden was a tiresome, hot, and boring job! Mama and I would start working early morning, but long before the day's hoeing was finished, the sun would be overhead and hot. HOT! I had long since removed my long sleeve outer shirt, but Mama insisted I keep the big straw hat on my head. Oh, the sun was so hot! I couldn't wait to get back in the house!

In addition to the unbearable heat, numerous honeybees buzzed around the garden. They buzzed around the plants, around my legs, even, occasionally, near my face.

"I despise bees!" I declared to Mama, as I swatted at one of the pesky things.

"Those little creatures are a blessing to our garden," Mama told me. "Without them, it would be almost impossible to have a garden, because they pollinate the vegetables. For example, squash. The very first blooms in the center of the squash plant stands straight up. These are the male blooms. The next blooms lay in a circle around the upright blooms. These are the female blooms. The bees visit the male bloom, collect the pollen on their legs, then visit the female blooms, and this pollination is absolutely necessary for the squash to produce their delicious golden fruit. (See, God has a plan, a purpose for everything.) Even the little honeybee has a very important place in God's creation."

I was glad the honeybees pollinate the squash. I liked squash. But I still didn't want the things flying anywhere near me. They could at least wait until I was inside the house to come to the garden! The garden wasn't big enough for the two of us at the same time!

A "bobwhite", sitting on a tree limb at the edge of the woods, kept calling, "Bob-white - Bob-white", oh, how I would love to be a bird and not have to work in the garden in the hot sun. I would trade places in a second with that bird!

Finally, at 11 o'clock, Mama left the garden to cook a large meal, enough for both dinner and supper. I was given freedom and escaped the garden.

By the middle of May, the first garden's green peas, beets and carrots were ready to harvest and preserve. By July 1st, the second garden's vegetables were in full production and ready to harvest. This, added to the cultivation each garden required and all the regular work Mama did each day, resulted in twelve-hour days for her.

Daddy had purchased a large pressure canner for Mama. The canner held five half gallon jars or seven-quart jars at a time. The canner cut down on the time needed to process the vegetables, but not on the heat from the woodstove to bring the pressure in the canner up to ten pounds and hold it for twenty-five minutes.

Mama kept a constant check on the fire in the stove, on the canner, and on the canner's pressure, making sure the three worked together correctly. Mama often heard of housewives whose canner had gotten too hot and blew up, many times to cause severe injuries to her and her kitchen. Mama's careful observation and oversight kept herself and her kitchen safe all the years of her canning.

The hot days of July through September, with the woodstove heating for eight straight hours a day from Mama's cooking our daily meals and from canning, made the house unbearably hot and stuffy. All the doors and windows were opened wide to allow any breeze to flow through the rooms, and this, slightly helped relieve the smothering heat. Between rains, as the heat built up, the house was so hot, it was nearly impossible to sleep at night. I would lay in bed, covered in sticky perspiration, totally miserable. I was always glad when a rain came, even if it meant a thunderstorm, at least the days were cooler after the storms had passed.

By July 10th, Mama and I would gather the beans/peas in the early morning, then take the baskets of vegetables to the backyard under the huge maple tree. Mama and I gathered around the baskets and worked amicably together in preparing the vegetables for canning.

Oh, how I enjoyed this time with Mama. I had her all to myself. She shared her childhood memories. She sang old Irish songs. She told me the latest stories and articles she had read in the ladies' section of the Progressive Farmer magazine. She taught me many life lessons with her timely and profound advice. Mama's lessons were easy to learn and immaculate because she taught them by living them and being the example of her own teachings.

I also treasured this time with Mama because working with her preparing food for the family, made me feel productive, appreciated, and "grown up".

Tomatoes, squash, fruits, and corn couldn't be prepared outside. They had to be prepared in the kitchen. The vegetables, the corn, particularly, had to be prepared and canned as swiftly as possible the day it was harvested. When canning tomatoes, Mama always kept the seeds. She cut the tomatoes into quarters and used her thumb to remove the pulp section containing the seeds. She placed the sections into a large pot, then I would rub the mucilaginous pulp between my hands and place the seeds into a a vessel containing cold water. Next, I would stir the seeds, then churn them around and around and play with the pulp until I was tired of the game. Mama would skim off the top pulp, drain the seeds, then take the seeds to the attic and spread them out onto a board to dry. Two or three days later when the seeds were thoroughly dry, Mama would bring the seeds back to the kitchen. She rubbed the seeds between her hands with some fine sand, which freed the seeds from all traces of dry mucilage. She stored them in glass containers.

Daddy would gather the corn from the garden, bring it to the edge of the yard, near the fence, to remove the husks. He would throw the husks over the fence for the cows and chickens to fight over. The chickens, especially, loved scratching through the scraps for the fat worms that occasionally infested the corn. Boy, the chickens would chase each other for those scrumptious delights.

Mom and Daddy's diligent work combined with numerous rains throughout the growing season, enabled Mama to can over 700 quart and half gallon jars of fruits and vegetables. The jars were carried to the dirt basement under the north corner of the house and stored on the shelves. In addition to the canned fruits and vegetables, baskets of potatoes were allowed to dry for 3-4 days, then placed in wooden boxes and stored on platforms in the basement. In December, the baskets were covered with two layers of old quilts to help prevent the potatoes freezing

166

should the weather drop to 10 degrees or below during the winter months. In addition, apples and pears were wrapped individually in pieces of old newspapers (that Hazel, our neighbor had passed on to Mama.) and stored in baskets there also.

The summers the garden received a good weekly rain – the garden along with Mama and Daddy's persistent work produced a bountiful table for the family. Raising a large garden required a huge investment in work and time, but still did not take ALL the family's attention.

"Monday is always wash day; rain, shine, freezing cold, whatever the weather, Monday is wash day!" Mama declared.

There were days after a rain when the ground was too wet to work in the garden. Plus, there were many, many other jobs the house, animals, and farm required that kept the family from the garden.

Two-year-old Jacob was just as busy as the rest of the family. He was walking, running, feeding himself, learning to talk and already had a great sense of humor. He followed behind Daddy every day. He played games with me, and he entertained himself with his toys. He was a true delight to all of us.

But I had observed that most of the peaches were NOT being bought, and I couldn't understand why people weren't coming and buying the peaches. They were delicious!

I noticed that Daddy didn't laugh or joke as much as he used to, in fact, he didn't even converse as before and that he seemed to be sad, very sad.

AUNT SADIE

In the south, during the 1940's company (guests) would drop in without previous notification. They often surprised us with their unexpected visit and caught us

167

unprepared. This was one of Aunt Sadie's (daddy's aunt but we all called her "aunt") habits: to drop in, unexpected at mealtime, hungry and ready to eat.

Aunt Sadie never married and worked at Mount Airy's only upscale, ladies' department store for 15 years. She stood five foot ten and kept her hair tied in a knot at the nap at her neck. She wore dark colored dresses, ankle length, straight and plain. Her little smiles never seemed to reach her eyes, and whenever she laughed, which was seldom, it sounded hoarse, as if she might have a sore throat. With her nose high in the air, everybody thought she was serine and sophisticated, but to me, she just seemed downright uppity, and of all the times she visited our family, I don't recall she ever once looked at or spoke to me. She was above such a thing, I suppose. Aunt Sadie's only redeeming grace as far as I was concerned, was her porcelain complexion and that she always smelled good, which was accomplished, I was certain, with her store-bought creams and colognes.

By the 1940's, Aunt Sadie had purchased a Ford Coup. She was among the first women in our area to drive, and the ONLY woman in our entire community to have her own car. Every Thursday evening, all the stores in town closed at 1 P.M. and her favorite thing to do after work was to take a leisure drive in the country, and the mountains surrounding our area. While out, she often visited one of her cousins, nieces or nephews and their families. None of us knew where her fancy might take her or when she might visit.

Well, as was her habit, one Thursday, out of the clear blue sky, Aunt Sadie dropped in at 6 P.M, just as we had finished eating. Mama always cooked a large mid-day meal with plenty left over for our supper, but this evening we had eaten nearly all the food; all that remained was cornbread and three green tomatoes.

"Fried green tomatoes?" Aunt Sadie scuffed. "Whoever heard of such a thing?" when Mama offered to fix this treat for her.

"We like them." Daddy replied.

"But FRIED GREEN TOMATOES? Why, that's like fried watermelon, or cantaloupe, or even cucumbers!" she insisted, "Do you fry them too?" she squeaked.

"Oh, really, Aunt Sadie, you should try them. Lena makes them extra special," Daddy protested.

"Well, I could just eat some of your cornbread and buttermilk," she replied, half-heartedly.

Mama was tired from her daily labor, but she told Aunt Sadie, "I can cook you some potatoes or some beans."

"No, no. Don't go through any trouble for me." Aunt Sadie pouted.

Daddy, in his final attempt to appease Aunt Sadie, "Just try these tomatoes first, Aunt Sadie." he almost pleaded. "You just might be surprised."

"I prefer my tomatoes red, ripe, sliced, and chilled, not hot, green, and fried," Aunt Sadie haughtily replied.

Mama removed the cornbread, still warm from the stove's warming hood to the table. She also set out a glass pitcher of milk and a small bowl of chopped onion. She then, quickly, rekindled the fire in the stove and within minutes had fried the tomatoes, and served them piping hot to Aunt Sadie.

We all sat down to watch Aunt Sadie eat. She took a tiny bite, chewing with her front teeth only, ready to spit the food out if necessary. She took a larger second bite and chewed it more slowly. But the third bite was a huge mouthful and then she quickly consumed the entire plate of FRIED GREEN TOMATOES.

When she looked up and caught us staring at her, our mouths open in amazement; she politely wiped her mouth and haughtily inquired, "Haven't any of you ever seen a lady eat fried green tomatoes before?"

For the first time ever, I thought I saw a smile in her eyes. But Aunt Sadie's mouth dropped open when Mama smugly replied, "If you like them, just wait til you taste my Green Tomato Pie!"

Irish Blessing

May You Always Walk In Sunshine
May You Never Want For More.
May Irish Angels Rest Their Wings Right Beside Your Door.

Sitting on the front porch, Daddy asked me: "What is it?" For clues to the answer, he said: "I found it---- I picked it up---I hunted for it---Couldn't find it---So, I threw it down and then, I walked off with it. What is it?" All four daughters and even Mama offered suggestions as to its identity. None of us came up with the correct answer. "A splinter in your foot".

How to Preserve a Husband

Be careful in your selection. Do not choose too young. When selected, give your entire thoughts to preparation for domestic use. Some wives insist upon keeping them in a pickle, others are constantly getting them into hot water. This may make them sour, hard, and sometimes bitter, even poor varieties may be made sweet, tender, and good, by garnishing them with patience, well sweetened with love and seasoned with kisses. Wrap them in a mantle of charity. Keep warm with a steady fire of domestic devotion and serve with peaches and cream. Thus, prepared they will keep for years.

Darling, You Can't Love But One

I'm leaving on that New River Train,
I'm leaving on that New River Train.
Riding the same old train that brought me here,
    And it's sure going to carry me away.

O darling, you can't love but one,
O darling, you can't love but one.
O darling, you can't but one and have any fun,
    O darling, you can't love but one.

O darling, you can't love two,
O darling, you can't love two.
O darling, you can't love two and still be true,
    O darling, you can't love two.

O darling, you can't love three,
O darling, you can't love three.
You can't love three and still love me,
    O darling, you can't love three.

O darling, you can't love four,
O darling, you can't love four.
You can't love four, and love me anymore,
    O darling, you can't love four.

O darling, you can't love five,
O darling, you can't love five.
You can't five, and get honey from my beehive,
    O darling, you can't love five.

O darling, you can't love six,
O darling, you can't love six.

You can't love six, and still love Saint Nix,
O darling, you can't love six.

O darling, you can't love seven,
O darling, you can't love seven.
You can't love seven, and go with me to heaven,
O darling, you can't love seven.

Oh, I'm leaving on that New River train,
Oh, I'm leaving on that New River train.
The same old train that brought me here,
Is going to carry me away.

CHRISTMAS

The week before Christmas each year, we searched the woods surrounding our home for a white pine Christmas tree. Some years, 2 or 3 searches were required before we found a tree that met our hopeful expectations. The tree was placed in the living room inside a bucket. Rocks were tightly stuffed around the tree trunk, holding the tree secure. We decorated the tree with strings of colored rope and shiny foil icicles. Mama allowed an old quilt to be laid under the tree.

The past year, (my first grade), I saved all my colored work papers, and these I cut into 2x2 and 3x3 inch squares. Mama gave me the thread and the use of a needle to string the squares two inches apart on the thread. I even drew pictures of Santa on some of the squares to help with the tree decoration.

Last year, the first back at school after the Christmas break, all the girls had brought their favorite gift Santa had given them to share with their classmates. ALL of them had received the NEW soft faced vinyl baby dolls. The dolls were dressed in pink infant's clothes, a bonnet, and pink booties. They were BEAUTIFUL! So soft, so precious, so REAL looking! No more hard-cold faced dolls for me I promised myself. I had never really liked the hard-faced dolls, now, I understood why, they were FALSE looking!

I told Mama about the new doll numerous times through the coming year and that the new doll was ALL I wanted Santa to bring me for the coming Christmas. I couldn't wait to hold and care for my own "baby". The last 3 days before Christmas, time slowed down to a crawl, each minute seemed an hour long, each hour was a day long. Would Christmas morning ever arrive? It seemed time had completely STOPPED!

On Christmas Eve morning, Mama was in the kitchen preparing a large dinner for Christmas Day. I had the job of standing by the cookstove and constantly stirring the pie filling to prevent it from sticking to the pan and from forming lumps. A very important responsibility, and I always met Mama's strict instructions and received her approval, and her "Thank You".

Mama made the pie crust and whipped the egg meringue with a hand beater. To get the high, fluffy peaks, she would beat the egg whites for an hour, sometimes longer. Mama then placed the pies in the oven until the meringue was evenly browned.

Mama seasoned all her pies and cakes with Raleigh extracts. The Raleigh salesman came to our house 2 or 3 times a year. He carried a large basket full of samples he was selling. Mama did not have money to buy any of the products—except for the extracts. Mama said Raleigh's was the best of its kind, and the family truly agreed, for Mama's pies and cakes were always delicious.

Christmas Eve night, I hardly slept any, I was so anxious to hold my new baby doll! Finally, about 4 AM, unable to wait any longer, I rose quietly from my bed and tiptoed to the living room. With no fire burning in the fireplace, the room felt as cold as ice, but I didn't care, the new baby and I would return to my bed where it was warm. I pulled the light string and looked around for my doll. I didn't see it immediately, so I turned around and around still looking. I looked behind the couch and chairs, even behind the tree. No doll. There WAS a 10-inch hard-faced doll lying on one end of the couch along with 6 oranges, and a small stick of peppermint candy. Oh, I couldn't believe my eyes! Santa had brought me the same doll he had brought last Christmas! How could he do that? I started crying with overpowering disappointment. I tiptoed back to my bed and under the covers, I continued to softly cry.

Then, suddenly, I understood why Santa did not bring my doll. --- I must have been too naughty sometime during the past year to receive the doll. (Children were often told Santa was watching to see if they were naughty or nice.) I slept late that morning. I did not return to the living room or touch the doll. It laid where Santa had placed it. However, Santa did bring my little brother the small tricycle he had asked for. I was glad for him.

On New Year's Day, I finally could speak to Mama about the doll without crying. "Why didn't Santa bring me the doll I asked for, Mama?"

"Santa didn't have the money to buy it. The new baby doll cost 4 times more than the regular doll, so he brought it instead. He didn't know you would be so disappointed with it, she explained. But I was disappointed—terribly disappointed—But I never played with the doll a single time. I had suddenly outgrown dolls and I NEVER asked Santa for a doll again.

Jacob Jr. peddled his tricycle across the back porch, back and forth, in and out, into the kitchen, did a wide circle in the floor, back to the porch over and over, round and round.

With warmer weather, Jacob and I took the tricycle outdoors to the driveway. He sat on the seat, me, with one

174

foot on the deck, pushed the two of us along with my other foot, all the way down the long driveway, back and forth, up, and down, the driveway for hours at a time. Finally, after months of this constant treatment, the tricycle broke apart. We would put it back together, but it would soon break again, but we managed to get a year of steady playing out of it, which we both fully enjoyed.

- *Jacob Jr. and I standing in the backyard*

1948

Daddy decided to sell his small, blocky, awkward bulldozer as it was no longer needed. The last time the dozer had been used was in the farthest field from the house, and there it still set. Daddy didn't know if the thing would even start, much less to drive to the house. After several tries, the motor came to life.

Daddy slowly, loudly, with smoke rolling out the exhaust, drove the dozer toward the house, while I walked several yards behind.

Everything was going smoothly, until the dozer came to the three-foot drop between the field and the narrow roadway leading to the house. Suddenly, quicker than the blink of an eye, the dozer flipped on its side, and in the same instant on over on its top, pinning Daddy completely under it!

I screamed loudly. I knew the two-foot-high iron gearstick had pierced Daddy in the chest, pinning him to the ground under it!

I screamed hysterically; THIS accident had killed Daddy for SURE!

Finally, able to move, I ran to Daddy as quickly as I could, to see his head poking out from the narrow strip between the ground and the side of the dozer. He had landed in the bottom of the three-foot ditch, and the tracks on each side of the dozer had landed on the sides of the ditch, keeping the weight of the dozer from crushing Daddy.

"Thank you, Jesus! Thank you, Jesus!" I sobbed as Daddy slowly, very slowly, squeezed his way from beneath the dozer.

After several days, the soreness all over Daddy's body was beginning to ease, so he hitched the horses' harnesses to the side of the dozer. The horses pulled the dozer to its side, then quickly and easily flipped it upright.

Daddy cranked the dozer and drove it to the back yard as the horses followed behind.

A month later, as the new owner drove his truck down our driveway with the dozer loaded on its bed, Daddy stood in the yard, relieved to be rid of the monster.

I stood in the yard, too, rejoicing that Daddy was still here with his family, alive and well!

Orchard

Dad had done everything "by the book":

- He had carefully studied the growing of peaches and all the steps required to make a productive orchard
- He had taken months to clear the land of scrub trees, bushes, and stumps
- He had worked to remove stumps and roots from the ground
- He had plowed the land deeply
- He had allowed the plowed fields to set, giving the top soil time to soften
- He had covered the fields in hundreds of pounds of limestone to sweeten the soil, to ensure sweet peaches
- He had hauled wagon loads and loads of cow manure from his brother-in-law's dairies to enrichen the fields
- He had chosen the correct variety of peaches to grow for his area
- He had sowed the fields in grasses to help control weeds and to hold the soil during heavy rains

- He planted the seeds at the correct depth
- He had watered the young trees, the first two years, during dry spells to ensure each tree received all the moisture they needed to form roots and grow, and not a single tree had perished.
- He had fertilized the trees with both nitrogen and potassium, 1/2 of it one month before bloom, the second half after the young peaches had started to develop each spring
- He sprayed the orchard each spring and early summer with expensive insecticides and herbicides to keep insects and leaf diseases away from the trees
- He had kept the orchard mowed and weed free
- He had pruned each tree every winter to open up the interior of the tree
- Again, forty days after bloom to remove any new upright shoots arising at the trees' interior, to enable both sunlight and rain to reach the growing peaches
- He had accomplished the tedious and time-consuming task of removing the excess blooms by dragging a rope over and through the tree limbs
- Again, forty days later, after the small peaches started to grow, to remove the excess small peaches, ensuring large peaches, and to prevent overworking the trees by their heavy production.
- He had, each winter, picked up rocks from the orchard and fields and hauled them by the wagon loads to fill in the soft, muddy places in the long driveway leading to our house. He didn't want our customers to get their vehicles dirty.
- He had made hundreds of wooden bushel sized baskets to pick the peaches into and for truckers to haul the peaches away

- He had "talked" peaches to EVERYONE- from Mr. Bowman at the FHA to Mr. Sawcett at the bank, to church members at the Primitive Baptist Churches he attended
- To brothers and brother-in-law's, to neighbors, to friends, to acquaintances on the street
- To fruit stand owners, to truckers, to store managers, to wholesalers, even to Surry Dairy to make peach ice cream.
- To café and restaurant owners
- He had advertised in both Mount Airy News and Times, on WPAQ radio, even Stuart and Winston-Salem newspapers
- He had mailed flyers to large canneries
- He had, the last thing before going to bed each night, and first thing each morning, asked God as humbly and reverently as he knew how to please bless his endeavor

He had done everything "by the book". The result was big, juicy, delicious peaches on every tree, over 7,000 bushels a year, except for the years a killing freeze had destroyed the crop.

Daddy had worked. He had toiled and labored for 13 long, long years. Daddy had succeeded. His orchard was by far, the best producing, best tasting peaches in the entire area.

Daddy just couldn't sell his peaches. That was Daddy's only failure. Daddy was unable to sell the peaches in the huge quantities the orchard produced, and the amount needed to pay for the land, the expense of growing the orchard, the First National Bank, the Farmers Home Administration, and Milt Warden. Daddy, by being unable to sell the peaches, had failed to provide a living for his family, to give his wife and his children the normal things that a family needed and wanted. The orchard was a failure!

Dad just wanted to crawl in a hole and hide. All his work, all his dreams, for nothing. NOTHING! He didn't have enough money to buy a pair of shoes for his young son.

Then, in early August, Ray Dowell came to our home. After talking with Daddy and agreeing upon a price per bushel, Ray ordered a truck load of peaches. Five hundred bushels!

Ray informed Daddy he was going to Richmond to take orders for the peaches and would be back in five days to collect them. Ray said, "I can sell these peaches to stores and road side stands all over the place between here and there. Just have them picked and ready. I'll be back."

Daddy's dream of filling large orders had finally come to fruition! When Ray sold this load, Daddy was certain, Ray would want more- maybe two or three more loads. Ray was a well-known trucker. He would probably know other wholesalers and truckers that would order large truckloads also as soon as Ray introduced them to Daddy.

Finally, the orchard would start paying and Daddy would be able to pay all his debts. Boy, how nice that would be---not to be in debt! Daddy hired Louis and Freddy Tolhart, our closest neighbor's boys, and we all started picking peaches early next morning. Mama and Daddy picked rapidly and efficiently, filling their peck buckets, then gently pouring the peaches into the baskets on the horse drawn wagon.

The boys picked more slowly, often stopping to take a drink of water from the fresh supply Mama had provided.

I picked my first bucket rapidly too. My second bucket a little slower. My third bucket took longer, because by now the peach fuzz was in the cruck of my arm and it was itching. I hated peach fuzz. I picked another bucket. Now, the fuzz was under my neck and itching me to death! I would pick a peach, then scratch. Pick one more, take longer to scratch! Finally, I was scratching far longer than I was picking! Oh, how I hated peach fuzz!

There was a huge, ripe, red peach just over my head, just begging me to eat him. The peach was calling my name, saying "come eat me. I'm juicy and good." I did. I ate him and of course, no one can eat just one of those scrumptious delights. I had to have another one. Then the third, even maybe a fourth! Now, I was itchy and sticky and so full of peaches I was about to bust open! The fuzz was driving me insane! I was scratching full-time now. I LOVED eating peaches! I HATED the fuzz.

The 5th morning of picking and with nearly 400 bushels picked, Ray Dowell returned to our home. Ray returned to cancel the order he had placed with Daddy four days earlier.

"Mr. Mosley," he explained, "I drove all the way to Richmond. I stopped at stores and stands in Danville, South Hill, South Boston, and I even went to the naval base at Norfolk, trying to locate buyers for your peaches. I was able to get only five small orders and that's not enough to pay the expense of me delivering the peaches to those stores.

"I'm sorry, Mr. Mosley, but I'll have to cancel my order. This year is just like all the other years, the market is flooded with peaches! The peach orchards in Georgia and North and South Carolina come in early and flood the market with their little cheap peaches. Then, all the orchards in Virginia and Maryland come in shortly after, and the market is just flooded. Orchard growers around here can't even give their peaches away. It's a shame, that's what it is, Mr. Mosely. It's a shame you can't sell your peaches. I'm sorry, but I don't know what to do, but cancel my order. I'm sorry for any inconvenience I caused you."

"I understand Ray," Daddy told him "I appreciate your trying to sell the peaches and coming to tell me you couldn't. Maybe next year."

Dad paid the two Tolbert boys the money he owed them and explained he wouldn't need them any longer, which was okay with the teenagers. They didn't like the fuzz either.

Daddy, with his head bowed and shoulders slumped, walked to the house. Without speaking, Daddy entered the middle bedroom, pulled the two dark green roller shades all the way to the bottom of each window, closed the two doors, making the room dark as night. Next, Daddy removed his shoes, laid down in the bed, then pulled the cover up to his chin.

All hope was gone- all hope that he could provide financial security for his family- all hope that the peaches would pay his debts- all hope for a better tomorrow.

The numerous baskets of picked peaches were rotting. The peaches were dropping from the trees, just to lay there and rot. "The rot matches my hopes, my dream, for a financially secure future for my family. My dreams are rotting away with each peach!" he said.

Mamma worked 18 hours a day every day, except Sunday. She kept the house up to her "spick and span" standards. She cooked two meals a day. Mama even did the strenuous job of providing wood for the cook stove for all the cooking and canning she was doing. Mama milked the cows twice a day. She tended the garden, gathered food to serve her table and preparing it to can. She helped the regular customers with their two or three bushels of peaches they purchased for their own family's consumptions.

Regardless of her long workday, Mamma would visit Daddy in his darkened room two or three times a day. Mamma would take food and water, "Please, try to eat a little and drink some water", she softly coached Daddy.

But Daddy could only take a bite or two. His appetite was completely gone. His desire to live gone. Mama continued her daily visits. She would tell Daddy about the latest customer or something cute their small son had said or done.

Daddy wasn't interested, his mood as black as midnight.

Mama said, "Please Jacob, come outside, it's a beautiful day."

Daddy remained silent, his face frozen, unable to speak or even smile. Mama said, "Please Jacob, the family needs you."

All the years of back breaking work, all the sacrifices the family had endured for the orchard- was for NOTHING! Lying in the dark, Daddy kept his hands over is ears, trying to stuffle the sound of ripe peaches hitting the ground. Daddy kept his eyes tightly closed, trying not to see the ground covered in big, juicy peaches, slowly rotting. Daddy tried not to think of the bushels of picked peaches at the edge of the yard that were unsold and rapidly decaying.

Daddy's days were long, black, empty, sad, full of guilt and remorse. His nights, even more torturous, endless and gut wrenching. Daddy's defeat was total and complete; he was devastated beyond words to express. Daddy's dreams, his hopes, his ambition were totally and finally destroyed. The peach orchard was a failure as far as providing an income for the family, and financial security for his children.

Daddy was so devastated, he considered killing himself, Mama and his two younger children. The four would be better off if they were dead and out of this world of pain, sorrow, bitter disappointments and heart aches. Yes, the four would be better off dead!

"I'm so melancholy I could just die," Daddy told Mama when she visited him in his darkened room. "I just feel like lying down in the orchard, and let the peaches fall on me- and cover me up- and just ROT! ROT! ROT! Away with them! The smell of rot is on the land, in the air surrounding this place, even in this room. It's permanently in my nose. It's deep in my spirit!

Mama's daily visits with Daddy continued into weeks as she patiently and tenderly encouraged Daddy to return to his family.

Wayfaring Strangers (song)

I'm just a poor wayfaring stranger
Traveling through this world below
There is no sickness, no toil, nor danger
In that bright land to which I go
I'm going there to see my Father
And all my loved ones who've gone on
I'm just going over Jordan
I'm just going over home
I know dark clouds with gather round me
I know my way is hard and steep
But beauteous fields arise before me
Where God's redeemed, their vigils keep
I'm going there to see my Mother
She said she'd meet me when I come
So, I'm just going over Jordan
I'm just going over home
I'm just going over Jordan
I'm just going over home.

But not all the peaches fell to the ground to rot. The entire back fields of the orchard next to the woods were picked clean of peaches, each and every year. One year, our neighbors, a father and his two adult sons politely helped themselves to all the peaches they wanted to make peach "white lightening".

Daddy's peaches were delicious for eating off the tree, to make pies and preserves, to can, and to make liquor, judging from the large volume of peaches the men took each year.

Starting in early August, two or three evenings a week, after it was completely dark, two or three vehicles, with their lights shining, came by our house, then slowly traveled the narrow drive through the orchard, until they reached the last fields of peach trees. There, they unloaded the buckets and baskets from their pick-ups and picked peaches until all their vessels were filled.

Loading the peaches back on the trucks, they then, moved on until they reached the woods on the other side of Daddy's land, then through the woods to Lovill Creek.

There under the huge canopy of crape myrtle bushes, over which stood huge oak trees, to block the liquor steel from exposure and its smoke, the men set up their steel making equipment.

Their thievery went on every week until all the peaches were competently gone. Their theft and the situation aggravated Daddy enormously, but he remained silent.

I had asked Daddy before why he didn't visit the sheriff's office and tell the deputy what was going on, but Daddy informed me it was better to keep quiet about the situation. It was rumored these neighbors had burned two houses in recent years late at night when the families were asleep inside.

This was never proved against them, but victims from both families were sure it was the Harris vehicles that drove away from their home those nights. "Best to let them have the peaches, and keep peace with them, then to risk our home getting burned down," Daddy told me each time I asked.

So, the Harris men, in six short weeks, made far more money from Daddy's orchard, than Daddy could ever earn working honestly and year-round! "Oh, life can be so unfair", I thought.

1949

On April 3rd, a sunny Sunday morning, Daddy stepped from the darkened room into the yard. As the sun warmed him and he looked at the velvet blue mountains to the North, he began to feel better, his depression lifting.

Slowly, he walked through the field of trees nearest the house as if to tell the trees goodbye. The war was over! No longer would he fight to make a living from the orchard.

Returning to the kitchen, Daddy told Mama and me, "I'm finished with the orchard. I'm through with it. It has taken too much from all of us. It's cost me a painful back and my health, my hard work, my peaceful days and nights, my children the things they needed, and you- 8 years of working at the mill, - and for what? It certainly has not paid for itself- I'm in debt- at times, it's even made me doubt God's love for me- nothing, but nothing is worth what this orchard has cost."

"But what are you going to do?" Mama asked him.

"I'm no longer working to grow peaches, no longer fertilizing the land, no longer spraying the trees or keeping them pruned, no longer advertising for customers, no longer allowing the Harris men to upset me as they steal my peaches. I'm letting it all go. I'm free of it!" I am washing my hands of it!

"But how will we manage to survive with NO income at all?" Mama asked Daddy rather anxiously.

"I've been giving our situation serious thought." Daddy answered. I know we just cannot sit down and give up. We must "keep on keeping on" as the saying goes.

"Here's what I've been thinking. I have been studying raising beef cows. We have the pastures, the hay and corn fields already. Plus, I have experience with raising calves- (Molly's and Sweet Pea's each year). All that is needed is a barn built to house them during winter months. Plus, the barn will have a huge loft to house the hay for their winter feed.

"The old barn was falling apart when we moved here and is ready to completely collapse now. It needs to be replaced anyway. The new barn will contain stalls on each side for both horses and both cows, plus smaller stalls for the calves we will purchase. We will purchase 10 weaned male calves, 3 months of age each spring. After they have been here for 2 months, and are growing and doing well, I will have each one castrated. This is a necessity for calm, happy, fast-growing steers, and the best tasting beef. We will raise them until they are at least 20 months of age, then sell them in late fall when they will weigh the most after eating green grass all season.

"This yearly income will pay the land, tax, and barn payments, and buy the new calves each spring. I am hoping it will also pay for a better vehicle—our old car desperately needs replacing. A good used pick-up will be needed to bring the calves to our place and then take the steers to market."

"But, Jacob, are you sure you will be able to sell the steers?" Mama inquired.

"Yes, I believe we can sell the steers. The market for beef has steadily been increasing the past several years due to more and more men leaving farming and going to work at public jobs to earn a better living for their families.

So, they are purchasing their beef from grocery stores instead of raising the meat themselves. This is creating a ready market for beef. When the steers are 20 months old, I can take them to the Mount Airy Stock Market, which is open each Wednesday. Nearly every week, all the beef cows are being bought by beef processors. If a steer does not sell that Wednesday, it can be returned the following Wednesday to be sold.

This will require three, maybe four years to get into full production and have 10 beef steers for sell each fall. In the meantime, I have some other ideas for your consideration. One of them, we will have still had peaches to sell for the next two or three years, maybe more, until the trees become overgrown, disease ridden, and the peaches are full of worms. Until that time, I'll reduce the price from $1.00 to 50 cents a bushel and turn the orchard into a "pick-your-own!"

"In the meantime, I will begin to cut down the peach trees in the further fields. I will leave a three-foot-high stump on each tree that when a chain is wrapped tightly around it, near the ground, the horses, together, can pull the stump up and out of the ground. I will turn this cleared land into pastures or hay fields for the cattle. What are your thoughts on this idea?" Daddy asked.

"Absolutely!" Mama quickly answered. "Those neighbor men have stolen enough of your peaches. It's time to put a stop to their thievery!"

"Now, I have something else to tell you. While we are waiting for the barn to be built and more land cleared for the steers, we are going to need an income to get all this started and to pay our yearly land payment and tax bills.

"My last two visits to Mr. Bowman's office to discuss my financial difficulties, and how best to get myself out of the mess I put myself in, he has suggested to me on how I can save our beautiful place. He told me I can earn a lot of money on an 8-week job, each fall, from August 1st through October 1st. It will mean leaving you and the kids of course during this 8-week separation. Do you think you can manage ok? Should I take this job?"

"Oh, Jacob, I don't know."

"We will write to each other every other day to keep in close contact. You tell me everything going on the farm. Or, if an absolute emergency should occur, I can always come home."

"What is this job, Jacob, and where is it located?"

"Mr. Bowman has told me about several large tobacco farmers in Ontario, Canada, who are seeking experienced "leaf-curers" from Virginia, as their tobacco is similar to ours grown here. They are seeking experienced, reliable tobacco farmers with the expertise to cure the green leaves to a bright golden color and with all the stems cured completely dry. R.J. Reynolds and other cigarette makers purchase ONLY these leaves.

"Mr. Bowman said the job pays 3 times more in 8 weeks, than I've ever earned in 1 year with my peaches! Mr. Bowman said one tobacco grower is desperate for an experienced and reliable "curer" to help him save his farm before the bank there forecloses on his loan."

"Oh, that's sad," Mama said softly.

"This farm has a large one room house with a screened front porch near the barns for me to live in. This is provided at no cost to me. Also, at no cost, I'll be provided with both breakfast and dinner. The meals the wife prepares for her family will be shared with me and brought to me at the house 7 days a week. For supper, I'll be supplied with fruits and a sandwich, also at no charge. There is a well nearby for drinking and bathing water and an outhouse several yards below the barns. So, all my physical needs will be met.

"There are 8 barns in the middle of several large tobacco fields. The barns are set 4 in a row. The remaining 4 barns are directly across from the first 4, front to front, making it convenient to go from barn to barn.

"The wood for the fires to "cure" the tobacco leaves have been cut and supplied at each barn, plus more wood will be supplied as needed. All 8 barns will never need firing at the same time, for one or two will be in the process of being filled with newly harvested green leaves and at the same time, one or two of the barns will be full of cured leaves, waiting to be removed to the pack house. That leaves 4, maybe 5 at a time that will require my full attention, both night and day.

"Now", Daddy asked Mama. What are your thoughts on this?"

"Well, Jacob, we need the income, that's for sure. I am not the least afraid of being by myself with the children. We have wonderful neighbors if help should be needed for anything. You're the one taking a risk being surrounded by strangers on a bus for hundreds of miles and then living with strangers on their farm and in their care." Mama took a long, deep breath. She silently asked her Heavenly Father what she and Jacob should do. Then, in an instant, complete, and total peace, and calm spread through her spirit, and she knew, KNEW that their Heavenly Father would be with both her and Jacob during their separation to guide, protect, and comfort them.

"Jacob, you know Mr. Bowman can be trusted. He has truly had your best interests at heart. Whatever you decide, I will abide with your decision."

"If all goes well in Canada," Daddy replied, "I'd like to go there for the next 3 or 4 autumns to get the cattle business up and running smoothly without putting ourselves into another financial strain.

"Oh, I have one more suggestion. Since both Iona and Audrey have married and moved to their new homes, the cows are giving us more milk than we can use. This past summer, 3 different ladies who purchased our peaches, asked me if we have milk, butter, or buttermilk for sale. These women work at the mills in Mount Airy and live up the road from here. They will stop by on their way home once a week to pick up the items you have ready. This will give you 3 sales per week, and if you are willing, this money can be used to buy the groceries needed and pay the light bill. Any extra money is to be saved along with the peach money you will get while I am gone to be applied to painting the outside of the house. It needed painting when we moved here and with a big, new barn in the backyard, the house must be painted, so it will not look bad compared to it. We also need a heavy wood burning heater. The thin, tin heaters we have been using all these years, last only 4 or 5 years before they need replacing. A thick, heavy heater would hold heat much longer and would last for many years.

"What's your thoughts on all of this?" Daddy inquired.

"Yes, absolutely! The house desperately needs painting!" Mama exclaimed." I have been concerned about our surplus milk and what to do with it. I cannot stand to see it wasted. I can start selling this week if you'll let the women know."

"Excellent," Daddy replied.

"My only concern: I want us to continue to raise our gardens as usual."

"And that we will definitely do." Daddy firmly stated. "August, when I leave for this job, most of the garden work for me will be finished and the garden will not require my attention until the late fall plowing."

"I'll go to Mr. Bowman's office Monday to learn more about going to Canada. I will also need to sign the papers necessary to borrow the money to get the barn built."

Daddy rose from his seat. He gave Mama a long, tender hug, then a loving kiss of compassion and gratitude. "Thank you, my precious wife." Daddy said softly.

Daddy sat back down in his chair and after several minutes, breathed a deep sigh of relief. Then, with a look of relief and eyes full of joy, he said, "In my depression, I forgot that God, the great Jehovah, loves me and my precious family."

God has promised to be with us through both good and bad times, to be our comfort in times of sorrow and defeat, to carry us when the load is too heavy to bear. God loves us so much; He has stored all our tears in a bottle. He has buried all our sins in the sea of forgetfulness to be remembered no more. He promised the lightweight afflictions of this world carries a heavy weight of glory on the other side. To all who believe in Him and are called according to His purpose, He will give eternal life to be spent with Him and all the heavenly host for all eternity. We are His children, and He loves us equally as He loves His first-born son, our Lord and Savior, Jesus Christ.

"The Bible clearly states that man shall have trials and tribulation while on this earth. In fact, look at how Jesus Christ suffered while here. He committed NO sin, and done only good to everyone He encountered, and He constantly walked and talked with His heavenly Father and done His Father's will. No matter how rough life might get for us, our pains will NEVER compare to what Jesus suffered on this earth.

"Our trouble began in the Garden of Eden. God made the Garden of Eden for man, food for the gathering, peace loving animals, no rain or storms, perfect weather night and day, and most incredible Father God, our Heavenly Father dwelled with them in perfect harmony and peace. Adam and Eve were so sinless and pure, they did not even try to hide their nudity. But, then the serpent (Devil) asked Eve 'Did God REALLY say you would die if you ate from the tree of Life? You shall not surely die, for God doth know that day you eat thereof, then you shall be as gods knowing good from evil,' the serpent told her.

"So, Eve tasted the fruit and it was good to eat, plus it would make one wise. She took the fruit and also gave one to Adam and he ate the fruit also. After Adam and Eve disobeyed God, everything changed. God removed them from the Garden, the gates were locked to keep them out, and God cursed the animals and the earth."

God is STILL in complete control, but he has allowed the Devil to tempt, frustrate and torment all of mankind ever since. That's the reason mankind is tossed between light and dark, happiness and sorrow, up and down, wellness and sickness, right and wrong, and this will continue until Jesus returns to earth. He has promised He will lock the Devil up where he will not be allowed to torment us any longer. But, until the glorious day of His return, God the Father, Jesus our Savior, and the indwelling Holy Spirit are to be the MOST important part of our lives. He is to be MORE important than our money, our sicknesses, our aches and pains, our mistakes, our failures, even first over our beloved family and especially over ourselves," Daddy told Mama and me.

"God created Adam, the first man, from the dust of the ground and Eve from Adam's rib, but EVERY child since then, He has knitted together in their mother's womb. He knows each one and has a plan, a purpose for each life. In addition, He wants each one to spend all eternity with Him, starting here on earth. To help achieve this, He made an empty place in each heart/soul that He and He ALONE can fill. Nothing can fill that emptiness, not other people, children, money, drugs, sports, work, crime, sex, no, not anything can fill the void! Only, repeat: ONLY THE HOLY SPIRIT can fill the emptiness in one's soul. The indwelling HOLY SPIRIT brings comfort, wholeness, understanding, hope, and TOTAL PEACE with our

Heavenly Father, the Great Jehovah, God, and Maker of the universe!

"To be adopted as a TRUE child of God is a FREE gift. We can't buy it or earn it in any way, it is free through God's grace, mercy, and love, and Jesus' sacrificial blood on the cross which paid the death penalty for our sins.

"All we need to do is recognize we are sinners, and sincerely ask God to forgive us, pleading Jesus's blood."

Mama was relieved at Daddy's decision to let the orchard go and believed he had made a wise choice. She also felt very hopeful about his future plans. Yes, it was time to let go, and hopefully enjoy peace.

That summer, the peaches produced an abundant crop and the usual customers, if not more than usual, came and bought the peaches. Mama saved the money from the sales, every penny, and paid it on debts. The first and far most important debt Daddy paid with the money was to Milton Warden.

All the years Daddy cultivated the land, planted the trees and worked the orchard, Milton had extended credit to Daddy for the necessities the household needed.

Salt, coffee, flour, sugar, baking powder and baking soda, canning lids and rings, Dad's small bags of smoking tobacco, and the paper to roll cigarettes were the necessities Dad purchased on the credit Milton allowed him. The years had accumulated into a $236.26 bill.

I remember Mr. Ward, for his kindness and generosity to my brother and me, for when the two of us walked to Milton's store, for the two or three items Mom had sent us after, Milton would always, every single visit, give my brother and me a piece of candy or chewing gum, absolutely FREE! With a loving smile on his face!

Boy, how we loved those treats! In fact, Milton gave us our first cone of ice cream. I will always remember that cone of ice cream. It was a hot afternoon in late July, and Milton had just started selling ice cream in cones, so he gave my brother and me a cone each!

The ice cream started to melt inside the store, and outside as we slowly walked home, the ice cream melted faster than we could eat it, causing it to run all over our mouths and hands, even down our arms. We arrived home sticky, but happy. We had eaten ice cream! Thanks to Milton's loving kindness and generosity.

"That's okay," he would tell Daddy when he visited the store, concerned about his inability to pay Milton the money he owed him, and yet once again needing to get one or two items on credit.

"One of these days, that peach orchard of yours is going to pay big time and you'll be the richest man in the whole community," he had encouraged Daddy, "In the meantime, don't worry about your bill. I'm not. To me it's like having money in the bank. Safe and secure, because I know you'll pay me as soon as you're able to," he'd tell Daddy. "In the meantime, don't worry about it."

Daddy laid the money on Milton's counter as he counted it out- all he owed.

Milton's face lit up, more for Daddy's success than for being paid.

"See Jacob, haven't I been telling you all these years that orchard would pay off someday?"

"Yes, Milt, you certainly have," Daddy said, as he shook Milt's hand in friendship, respect, and brotherly love.

LATER

Standing in the backyard, looking over the green fields onto the velvet blue mountains in the background, Daddy and Mama agreed the Heavenly Father had given them one of the most beautiful places on earth to live. They both heartedly agreed, "you can look at what you don't have and be very poor, or look at what you do have, and be very rich! It's your decision."

• *Standing in the yard looking northwest*

• *Standing in the yard looking northwest*

Daddy said, "Observe how Christ loved us. His love was not cautious, but extravagant. He didn't love in order to get something from us, but to give everything of himself to us." (Ephesians 5:2).

"Yes, we're RICH! RICH! RICH! Rich beyond words to tell. Our TRUE riches are in Jesus Christ, and in Heaven we will be BOTH with Him and like Him for ALL eternity, forever and forever! And He could come at any moment for us! Oh, I can't wait to be with Him." Daddy's voice and face were full of love, joy, and peace. "Thank you, Heavenly Father, Son and Holy Ghost."

Rich? Or Poor?

Which are you?

Mama's Recipes

Mama was an excellent cook. She could take limited ingredients and make a delicious, nutritious meal with them. She was an excellent gardener too, growing nearly ALL our food. Thank you, Mama. Here are some of her favorite recipes through the years

Entrees

Lena's Chicken Soup

2 pounds chicken pieces
2 chicken bouillon cubes
2 carrots, thinly sliced
2 celery stalks, thinly sliced
4 medium-size potatoes, peeled and cut into bite size pieces
1 large onion, cut into pieces
1 teaspoon black pepper
2 tablespoons butter

1. Place chicken pieces in soup pot. Cover with water. Add bouillon cubes. Cover with lid.
2. Bring to slow boil over medium heat. Reduce heat and slow cook for 45 minutes or until meat falls from bones.
3. Allow to cool. Set pan in refrigerator overnight.
4. Remove pot from refrigerator.
5. Spoon hardened fat from broth surface. Remove meat. Discard skin and bones. Cut meat into   bite size pieces. Set aside.
6. Place carrots and celery in broth. Heat to boiling point. Lower heat and cook 5 minutes.
7. Add onions and potatoes. Cook chicken pieces until potatoes are tender, about 20 minutes.
    Cook additional 5 minutes.

Roast Turkey

1. Heat oven 350° F.
2. Remove contents from stomach and neck cavities.
3. Rinse turkey thoroughly in cold water.
4. Pat dry with paper towels.
5. Rub generously with cooking oil.
6. Place in a deep roasting pan.
7. Pour water into pan with turkey until nearly to top of pan.
8. Salt and pepper both bird and water, generously.
9. Cover tightly with lid.
10. Cook 20 minutes for each pound.
11. Take lid off last 30 minutes of baking, so turkey can brown.
12. Remove pan from oven and allow turkey to set in pan of cooking water (with cover on) for at least 1 hour.

Hamburger Casserole

1 lb. ground beef (90% lean)
1 lb. pork sausage
4 lbs. potatoes, peeled and sliced ¼ inch thick
1 large onion, sliced
1 tsp salt
½ tsp pepper
1 tsp beef bouillon granules
1 cup boiling water
1 28 oz. can dice tomatoes, undrained
Minced fresh parsley, optional

1. In a Dutch oven, layer half of the meat, potatoes, and onion.
2. Sprinkle with half the salt and pepper. Repeat layers.
3. Dissolve bouillon in water; pour over all.
4. Top with tomatoes.
5. Cover and cook over medium heat for 45-50 minutes or until the potatoes are tender.
6. Garnish with parsley if desired.

Chicken Wings

1 ½ lb. chicken wings
2 tbsp butter
½ tsp salt
1 cup water
½ cup soy sauce
½ cup red wine vinegar

1. Cut off and discard tips of chicken wings.
2. Cut wings at joint to form 2 pieces from each wing.
3. In large skillet, melt butter over medium high heat.
4. Add chicken wings.
5. Quickly brown wings, turning once.
6. Sprinkle with salt and pepper
7. Carefully add water, soy sauce, and vinegar to skillet.
8. Bring to boiling; reduce heat.
9. Simmer uncovered, for 25-30 minutes or until chicken is no longer pink, turning wings once.
10. Remove chicken wings from skillet.
11. Keep warm.
12. Continue cooking sauce to desired consistency. Pour sauce over wings.

Makes 12

Pan-fried Trout

4-6 trout fillets
1 cup buttermilk
Salt
¾ cup fine cornmeal
½ cup of flour
1 teaspoon black pepper
¼ teaspoon celery seed
Oil for frying

1. After cleaning the fish, set them in milk and keep them chilled until time to cook.
2. In a heavy cast iron frying pan, pour enough oil to cover the bottom.
3. Turn the oven to 200° and lay a cookie sheet inside. Place a wire rack on top of the cookie sheet.
4. While the oil is heating, mix the cornmeal, flour, and spices together. Let the oil reach 350° – a good test is to flick a little dry breading into the oil, and if it fizzles at once, you are good to go.
5. Once the oil is hot, sprinkle the trout fillets with salt and dredge them into the breading. Shake off the excess and gently lay into the hot oil. Fry until golden brown, about 2-4 minutes each side. As you fry additional fish, you may need to lower the heat at some point.
6. Once the fish is ready, move it to the oven while you cook the rest of the fish. Keeping the fried fish warm in the oven will keep it crispy. When they are all done, serve at once with your favorite coleslaw and cornbread.

Irish Corned Beef and Cabbage

4 ½ pounds corned beef brisket
1 onion, peeled and left whole
2 bay leaves
2 beef bouillon cubes
1 small head cabbage, cored and cut into wedges
6 large potatoes, quartered
4 large carrots, peeled and sliced
¼ cup chopped fresh parsley
2 tablespoons butter

1. In a 6-quart Dutch oven, place the beef brisket, onion, bay leaves, and salt. Fill the pot with water to cover everything plus one inch. Bring to a boil and cook 20 minutes. Skim off any residue that floats to the top. Reduce heat to a simmer and cook for 2-3 hours until meat can be pulled apart with a fork.

2. Once the meat is done, add the cabbage, potatoes, and carrots to the pot and simmer for an additional 15 minutes or until the potatoes are tender. Skim off any oil that comes to the surface. Stir in butter and parsley. Remove the pot from the heat.

3. Remove vegetables to a bowl and keep warm. Slice meat on the diagonal against the grain. Serve meat on a platter and spoon juices over meat and vegetables.

Traditional Irish Beef and Guinness Stew

6 ounces bacon, diced
2 pounds beef chuck
3 tablespoons all-purpose flour
2 medium-large yellow onions, chopped
3 cloves garlic, minced
4 medium firm, waxy potatoes cut in 1-inch pieces
2 large carrots, chopped in ½ inch pieces
2 ribs celery, chopped in ½ inch pieces
1 large parsnip, chopped in ½ pieces
1 bottle (1 pint) Guinness Extra Stout
1 cup strong beef broth
2 tablespoons Worcestershire sauce
¼ cup tomato paste
1 teaspoon thyme
1 teaspoon dried rosemary
1 ½ teaspoons salt
¼ teaspoon black pepper
2 bay leaves
Salt and pepper to taste

1. Cut the beef across the grain into 1-inch pieces. Sprinkle with some salt, pepper, and the flour and toss to coat the pieces. Set aside.
2. Fry the bacon in a Dutch oven or heavy pot until done then remove it with a slotted spoon, leaving the bacon drippings in the pan.
3. Working in batches and being careful not to overcrowd the pieces, generously brown the beef on all sides.
4. Transfer the beef to a plate and repeat until all the beef is browned.

Traditional Irish Beef and Guinness Stew
Continued

5. Add the onions and fry them, adding more oil if necessary, until lightly browned, about 10 minutes. Add the garlic and cook for another minute. Add the vegetables and cook for another 5 minutes.

6. Add the Guinness and bring to a rapid boil, deglazing the bottom of the pan (scraping up the browned bits on the bottom). Boil for 2 minutes. Return the beef and bacon to the along with remaining ingredients and stir to combine. (**At this point you can transfer everything to a slow cooker if you prefer.

Spiral Ham with Cranberry Glaze

1 bone-in fully cooked spiral sliced ham (8lbs.)
1 can (14 oz.) whole-berry cranberry sauce
1 pkg. (12 oz.) fresh or frozen cranberries
1 jar (12 oz.) red currant jelly
1 cup light corn syrup
½ tsp. ground ginger

1. Place ham on a rack in a shallow roasting pan. Cover and bake at 325° F for 2 ½ hours.
2. Meanwhile, for glaze, combine the remaining ingredients in a saucepan. Bring to a boil. Reduce heat, simmer, uncovered, until cranberries pop, stirring occasionally. Remove from the heat, set aside.
3. Uncover ham, bake 30 minutes longer, basting twice with 1 ½ cups glaze. Serve remaining glaze with ham.

Old-fashioned Meatloaf

1 lb. ground chuck
1 lb. ground pork
1 medium onion
¼ cup fresh breadcrumbs (from 2 slices of stale bread, ground)
2/3 cup milk
1 large egg
4 tablespoons ketchup
3 tablespoons Worcestershire sauce
1 ½ teaspoons fine sea salt
1 teaspoon garlic powder
¾ teaspoon pepper

Sauce
½ cup ketchup
3 tablespoons apple cider vinegar
3 tablespoons brown sugar

1. Preheat oven to 350° F. Put 1 tablespoon cooking oil into a cast iron pan.
2. Combine the meats in a large mixing bowl. Grate the onion over the meat with a box grater.
3. Add the rest of the meatloaf ingredients and mix lightly with a fork, being careful not to mash the ingredients together.
4. Shape the mixture into a loaf shape and place in pan.
5. Bake for 1 hour to 1 hour and 15 minutes.
6. Pour the sauce over the meatloaf, continue to cook for 6 to 7 minutes.
7. Remove the meatloaf to cool. Serve.

Deviled Eggs

Place 6 large eggs (use eggs that are two weeks old or older) in a pot. Gently pour boiling water over eggs to completely cover them by 1-inch. Gently boil eggs, uncovered for 12 minutes. Immediately transfer eggs into a bowl of ice water for 5 minutes. Remove eggs from water and remove the shells. Slice each egg down the middle. Place yolks into a bowl and mash with a fork.

Add:

sandwich spread or mayonnaise

salt and pepper to taste

1 teaspoon rice wine vinegar

2 tablespoons drained pickle relish

Place yolks into the eggs. Top each with a sprig of parsley.

Breakfast Eggs

3 eggs
½ tsp salt
dash of pepper
1 cup milk

1. Beat eggs until very light.
2. Add seasoning and milk
3. Pour into well-greased top of double boiler. Do not stir or remove cover for 15 minutes.

Cook about 20 minutes over boiling water.

Pickled Eggs

Use directions above to boil 12 eggs. Remove from water, allow to cool, then remove shells. Fill a large jar with the hard-boiled eggs. Boil the pickling ingredients in a medium saucepan. Cover, reduce heat to low, and simmer for 30 minutes. If making pink pickles, strain out the beets. Chill the liquid for 20 minutes, then pour it over the eggs and screw on the lid. Keep refrigerated up to one month.

Golden Pickling liquid

1 ½ cups cider vinegar

½ cup water

2 teaspoons brown sugar or honey

2 teaspoons pickling salt

1 teaspoon ground turmeric

1 teaspoon whole allspice

¼ teaspoon celery seed

1 cinnamon stick

Pink Pickling Liquid

2 cups cider vinegar

1 ½ cups water

½ brown sugar or honey

2 teaspoons pickling salt

1 teaspoon whole allspice

½ teaspoon whole cloves

1 cinnamon stick

4 small beets, trimmed and cut into quarters

Creamed Eggs

6 hard-boiled eggs
2 tbsp fat
½ onion
2 tbsp flour
2 cups milk
1 tsp salt
¼ tsp pepper
6 slices hot buttered toast

1. Remove the shells from the eggs and cut each egg into six pieces.
2. Heat the fat in a frying pan and cook the chopped onions with it for a few minutes until   yellow, but not brown.
3. Remove the onions, make a sauce of the fat, flour, liquid and season. When it thickens, add the eggs and onions, and when they are well heated, turn the mixture out onto the buttered toast and serve at once.

Eggs Scrambled with Cheese

1 tbsp butter
1 cup milk
1 tsp salt
¼ tsp pepper
Cayenne pepper
6 eggs, beaten slightly
1 cup grated or ground cheese
Unsweetened crackers

1. Melt butter, and milk, seasoning, and eggs.
2. Cook like scrambled eggs and when almost done, shake in cheese. Cook 2 minutes more.
3. Serve on toasted crackers.

Poached Eggs

1. Put into skillet about 1 tsp bacon grease
2. When piping hot, put in eggs.
3. Salt and pepper and quickly pour in 1 tbsp boiling water
4. Cover closely and in 1 minute, they will be poached by steam.

Sausage Balls

1 lb. pork sausage, room temperature
1 8 oz. shredded sharp cheddar cheese, softened
2 cups Bisquick baking mix
1 cup water

1. Work sausage and cheese together.
2. Add Bisquick and water to sausage mixture.
3. With hands, work mixture until completely blended.
4. Form into walnut size balls.
5. Bake in preheated 425° oven for 15 to 20 minutes.

Tomato Hamburger Soup

1 46 oz. can V8 juice
2 (16 oz. each) packages frozen mixed vegetables
1 lb. sausage, cooked and drained
1 10 ¾ oz. can condensed cream of mushroom soup, undiluted
2 tsp dried minced onion
2 beef bouillon cubes

1. In 5-qt. slow cooker, combine the first five ingredients.
2. Cover and cook on high for 4-5 hours or until heated through.
3. Season with salt and pepper.

NOTE-Vary the flavor of this soup each time you make it by using different blends of frozen mixed vegetables.

Crispy Baked Chicken Legs

3 to 3 ½ pounds chicken legs – skin removed. (To remove the skins – fold a cloth around the larger end of the leg, hold firmly in left hand, using right hand, pull the skin from the leg.
In a bowl, mix the coating:
1 ¼ teaspoon salt
1 teaspoon black pepper
1 cup (or more) all-purpose flour
2 teaspoons powdered chicken bouillon

1. In a cast iron frying pan, place ½ cup oil and ¼ cup butter. Allow to melt and pan to become hot over medium heat.
2. Turn oven to 350° – Place parchment paper in bottom of rimmed cookie sheet.
3. Starting with the largest legs, roll 5 into the coating. Place into hot fry pan. DO NOT overcrowd – to allow room for easy turning.
4. Turn each leg as it browns until legs are completely brown on all sides.
5. When legs are brown, place on one end of the prepared cookie sheet, then place sheet into oven.
6. Continue this process until all legs are brown, starting with the largest legs to the smallest. As soon as each pan of legs is browned (roughly 10 minutes) remove cookie sheet from oven, place the second batch of browned legs on it and swiftly return the pan to the oven.
7. When all legs are browned and placed in oven, cook for an additional 30 to 40 minutes.

Note: Additional seasonings (if desired) placed in the flour mixture:
1 teaspoon smoked paprika
1 tablespoon dried Italian seasoning
½ teaspoon hot pepper flakes

Delicious Short Ribs

3 lbs. lean beef short ribs
2 medium onions, cut into chunks
1 cup water
2 beef bouillon cubes
1 tsp. salt
½ tsp. cinnamon
3 medium size sweet potatoes peeled and cut into chunks
1 cup medium size prunes, about 24

1. In Dutch oven, brown ribs well on all sides, drain off fat.
2. Push ribs to the side of the pan, add onion and sauté until
   tender
3. Add water, bouillon cubes, sugar, and cinnamon, cover tightly
4. Bake in preheated 350° oven 1 ½ hours.
5. Add potatoes and prunes. Cover and bake 45 minutes longer or until meat and potatoes are tender. Makes 4 servings.

Seafood Chowder

Place into soup pot:
3 tbsp oil
½ cup chopped celery (1 stick)
½ cup medium onion, chopped
½ cup green sweet pepper, chopped
½ tsp. salt
½ tsp. black pepper

1. Cover and cook over medium heat for 4-5 minutes. Stir.
2. Add 2 cups water, 2 Wyler's chicken bouillon cubes, 2 potatoes, peeled and cut into cubes, 2   carrots chopped.
3. Cook additional 10-15 minutes or until potatoes are tender, then add 2 cups corn, 2 cups milk,
    1 15 oz. can of Mackerel, broken into pieces, do not drain. Stir. Heat until hot. Serve immediately.

Mama's Soup
(using today's ingredients)

Sautee 1 lb. sausage & 1 medium onion on medium heat. Separate meat into small pieces. Cook until meat is browned.
Add: 1 15 oz. can pinto bean
    1 15 oz. can of corn
    1 14.5 oz. can of diced tomatoes
    1 10 oz. can dice tomatoes with green chiles
Heat on medium until hot. Stir often. Ladle into individual soup bowls. Top each with: cheese, sour cream, and/or taco chips.

Vegetables/Sides

Bone Broth Recipe

2 lbs. Mixed bones
3 quarts water, plus more as needed to keep meat covered
2 tablespoons apple cider vinegar
1 large carrot, quartered
1 large onion, quartered

1. Preheat oven to 400°F.
2. Place bones in a colander, rinse thoroughly under cool water, then pat dry with towels. Arrange bones in a single layer on a rimmed cooking sheet. Roast bones for 30 minutes or until golden brown.
3. Transfer hot bones to a large stock pot, add the water and vinegar to cover and stir to combine. Cover and let set for 30 minutes.

Mama's Pinto Beans

Carefully look through 2 cups of pinto beans, removing any small stones and trash, then wash the beans using two separate waters. Place the beans in a large bowl. Pour in water until the water level is 2 inches above the beans. As the beans begin to swell, stir occasionally, and add more water as needed to keep the beans fully covered. Allow to soak overnight.

Next morning, drain the water from the beans. Place the beans into a cooking pot. Cover the beans completely with fresh water. Add 1-inch slab of fat back meat or a ham hock to the pot. Place a cover on the pot. Cook the beans on medium low for 2 hours or until the beans are tender. 20 minutes before the beans are fully cooked, place a peeled potato into the beans and cook until tender. Remove the potato and discard it. The potato makes the beans easier to digest. Salt and pepper the beans to taste. Add 1 tablespoon of brown sugar or honey and stir to blend.

Top individual servings with:
Butter
Chopped onion
Pickled relish
Chow chow
Sauerkraut

Fried Cabbage

1. Fry some fatback to eat with cabbage.
2. Leave 3-4 tbsp of drippings in frying pan.
3. Put pot of water on to boil.
4. Chop a cabbage head like kraut or slaw.
5. Dump chopped cabbage into boiling water til wilted(blanched).
6. Dip out into frying pan.
7. Add salt and pepper to taste.
8. Fry about 5 minutes.

*Can use 2 chicken bouillon cubes (instead of fatback, if desired) with water.

Lena's Corn on the Cob

Lena always boiled corn on the cob without removing all the husks. Corn was picked during the morning hours, while the corn was still cool. The outer ½ of the husks were removed completely and discarded. The inner husks were pulled back far enough to remove the silk and placed back over the corn ear. If occasionally (if needed) a string was tied around the corn to keep the husks in place. Put corn into a pot of boiling water and boil for 20 minutes. Remove from pot, remove remaining husks. Next apple butter, add salt and pepper to taste. Serve hot. Corn this way is much sweeter than when all the husks are removed before boiling. Delicious!

Green Beans

half gallon prepared fresh green beans
5 bacon strips, diced
1 large onion, chopped
½ cup chopped green pepper
2 tablespoons all-purpose flour
2 tablespoons brown sugar
1 tablespoon Worcestershire sauce
1 teaspoon salt
½ teaspoon pepper
½ teaspoon brown mustard
3-4 diced tomatoes, peeled, undrained

1. Cook beans in 1 cup water. Bring to boil. Cover. Turn heat to medium and cook until tender.
2. Meanwhile, in a skillet, cook bacon until crisp, remove bacon from pan, drain, onion, and green pepper over medium heat until bacon is crisp and vegetables are tender. Remove with a slotted spoon.
3. Add green pepper and onion to pan. Cook until tender. Remove with a slotted spoon.
4. Stir the flour, brown sugar, Worcestershire sauce, salt, pepper, and mustard into the bacon droppings until blended. Stir in tomatoes. Drain green beans and add to mixture.
5. Serve hot.

Sweet Potatoes with Apples

3 to 3 ½ lbs. sweet potatoes
2 tart apples, peeled, cored, and cut into ¼ inch rings
½ cup orange juice
¼ cup packed brown sugar
¼ teaspoon ground ginger
¼ teaspoon ground cinnamon
2 tablespoons butter

1. Place sweet potatoes in a large saucepan and cover with water. Bring to a boil. Reduce heat. Cover and cook for 30 minutes or until just tender. Drain and cool slightly. Peel and cut into ¼ inch slices.
2. In a greased 13 in. by 9 in. by 2 in. baking dish, alternately laying potatoes and apples. Pour orange juice over top. Combine the brown sugar, ginger, and cinnamon; sprinkle over potatoes and apples. Dot with butter.
3. Bake, uncovered, at 350° F for 35 to 45 minutes or until apples are tender and heated through.

Fried Green Tomatoes

Tomatoes
Flour
Shortening
Salt and pepper
Sugar

1. Sliced tomatoes about ¼ inch thick.
2. Coat each piece with flour.
3. Put in a skillet of hot melted shortening or butter.
4. Salt and pepper to taste.
5. Sprinkle a generous amount of sugar on each piece of tomato.
6. When brown, turn over and sprinkle more sugar.
7. Fry until brown.
8. Remove from the pan and allow to drain.
9. Serve hot.

Creamiest Cream Potatoes

6 Large Red Potatoes, peeled and sliced
1. Place into cooking pot, add water up to ½ of the potatoes
2. Add 2 Wyler's chicken bouillon cubes
3. Cover loosely to allow steam to escape, Cook on medium heat until potatoes are tender 20-25 minutes
4. Check the potatoes often the last 10 minutes of cooking time, water should be mostly absorbed, but do not allow potatoes to burn
5. Remove from heat. Add 1 stick of butter. Using a hand potato masher, work together until completely blended and smooth.
6. Add salt and pepper to taste.
7. Slowly stir in ½ to 1 cup fresh cream until potatoes reach the creaminess desired.

Salads

Potato Salad

6 medium red potatoes, unpeeled
1 ½ cup mayonnaise
1 tablespoon vinegar
1 tablespoon prepared mustard
1 teaspoon salt
¼ teaspoon pepper
½ cup pickled relish
½ teaspoon celery seed
1 medium onion, chopped
    4   hard boiled eggs, chopped

1. Heat ½ cup salt to 3 cups water to a boil. Add potatoes, cover and heat to boiling; reduce heat. Cook 30 to 35 minutes or until potatoes are tender. Drain. Cool slightly and cut into cubes (about 6 cups). Leaving peeling on.
2. Mix mayonnaise, vinegar, mustard, salt, and pepper in a 4-quart bowl. Add potatoes, celery and onions. Toss. Stir in eggs and pickled relish. Cover and refrigerate 4 hours.

Chicken Salad

4 cups cooked chicken cut into cubes
1 cup celery, chopped
½ cup sweet pickle cubes
¼ chopped green onion
¾ cup mayonnaise or salad dressing
3 hard-boiled eggs, chopped
1 tablespoon pimentos, chopped
Salt and pepper to taste
½ tablespoon poultry seasoning
½ cup pecan chopped
1 cup halved seedless grapes
Combine all ingredients together. Chill.

Breads

Cornbread for Dressing or Stuffing

1. Heat oven to 400° F.
2. Grease large iron skillet with shortening, place into oven to heat as you mix cornbread ingredients together. Pan MUST be hot before adding cornmeal mixture to ensure a crunchy crust.
3. Mix:
   2 ¼ cup self-rising yellow corn meal
   1 tablespoon brown sugar
   1 ½ cup buttermilk
   2 large eggs
   ¼ cup cooking oil
4. Pour mixture into skillet and return to oven. Cook until crust is brown, 20 to 25 minutes.
5. Remove from pan immediately and allow to cool.

Sausage Cornbread Dressing

1 pound pork sausage, cut into thin slices
5 cups crumbled corn bread
1/3 cup finely chopped onion
1 cup finely chopped celery
2 tablespoons chopped parsley
1 ½ teaspoon salt
1 teaspoon poultry seasoning
1 teaspoon sage
1 teaspoon black pepper
1 cup turkey juice from roast pan

1. Place sausage into skillet, cook over medium heat while stirring and mashing with fork to crumble.
2. Add onion and celery and cook until sausage is browned, and vegetables are crisp tender.
3. Remove from heat and drain off juices.
4. In large bowl, combine cooked mixture with remaining ingredients.
5. Stir in enough turkey juice from the roasting pan to moisten well.
6. Pour into greased casserole dish, pressing firmly into bottom of dish.
7. Cover. Refrigerate.
8. 30 minutes before serving, place covered into 350° oven for 15 to 20 minutes or until hot.

Morning Glory Muffins

Mix in bowl one:

4 cups all-purpose flour

2 cups sugar

1 teaspoon salt

4 teaspoons baking soda

4 teaspoons cinnamon

Mix in bowl two:

2 cups grated carrots

1 cup raisins

1 cup chopped pecans

1 cup coconut

3 apples (grated)

Mix in bowl three:

6 eggs, beaten

1 ½ cooking oil

1 tablespoon vanilla

Stir contents of bowl three into bowl one. Add contents of bowl two. Drop into greased muffin tins. Bake at 350° F for 35 minutes. Makes 3 dozen. Keep in refrigerator. Warm before eating.

Irish Rosie's Soda Bread

3 ½ cups all-purpose flour
½ cup sugar
½ teaspoon baking soda
2 teaspoons baking powder
1 teaspoon salt
1-pint sour cream
2 eggs
2 tablespoons caraway seeds (optional)
¾ cup raisins

1. Combine dry ingredients together in large bowl.
2. In a small bowl beat eggs and stir in sour cream.
3. Add the egg and sour cream mixture to the dry ingredients and stir with a wooden spoon (batter will be very thick).
4. Add raisins and caraway seeds and stir well with a wooden spoon or knead in with your hands.
5. Place batter in a greased 9-inch pan.
6. Dust the top with enough flour so that you can pat the batter like a bread dough evenly in the pan without it sticking to your hands.
7. With a knife, make a shallow criss-cross on the top.
8. Baked for 50 minutes in a preheated 350°F oven.

Nora's Yeast Rolls

½ cup water, room temperature
2 ½ teaspoons (1 packet) active-dry yeast
1 teaspoon plus ⅓ cup sugar, divided
1 cup cooked mashed potatoes - cooled
¼ cup milk
6 Tablespoons salted butter, melted and cooled
2 large eggs
2 ½ teaspoon minced fresh rosemary leaves
1 ½ teaspoon salt
4 ½ to 5 cups all-purpose flour

Topping:
¼ cup salted butter, room temperature
2 Tablespoons honey

1. In a bowl, combine the water, yeast, and 1 teaspoon of the sugar. Set aside for 5 minutes or until the mixture looks bubbly. If the mixture doesn't start to bubble, then your yeast has likely expired and its best to start over with new yeast.
2. Mix the dough, add remaining sugar, mashed potatoes, milk, butter, eggs, rosemary and salt to a bowl with the yeast mixture and stir with a spatula until smooth.
3. Add 4 ½ cups of the flour and mix until you form a shaggy dough. Knead by hand for 5-7 minutes until the dough is smooth, forms a ball and pulls away from the side of the bowl. (it's okay if the dough sticks to the bottom of the bowl) If the dough is still sticking to the sides after a few more minutes of

Nora's Yeast Rolls
continued

4. kneading, add a little more flour 2 tablespoons at a time.
5. Place the dough in a lightly greased bowl, cover with a towel and place somewhere warm for about 1 hour, or until the dough doubles in size.
6. Line a 13x9 inch baking pan with parchment paper and lightly grease the paper.
7. Turn the dough out onto a lightly floured surface and cut into 16 to 20 equal pieces. Roll the dough into small balls, and place seam side down in the baking pan.
8. Cover and let the rolls rise until fluffed and nearly doubled in size about 15 minutes, before the rolls are ready. Heat the oven to 350°F.
9. Bake the rolls for 20-25 minutes, or until rolls are golden brown on top.

10. In a small bowl mix together ¼ cup room temperature butter and 2 tablespoons honey until smooth. Brush tops of rolls with the mixture, then sprinkle with salt. Allow to cool.

Fried Cornbread Patties

1 tablespoon butter
1 cup cornmeal
¼ teaspoon salt
1 tablespoon sugar
1 teaspoon baking powder
1 egg, slightly beaten
½ cup buttermilk

1. Place the butter into an iron skillet. Cook at medium high, allowing the butter to melt and the pan to get hot.
2. Meanwhile, stir the other ingredients together until well blended.
3. Drop 1 tablespoon of batter into the hot pan.
4. Cook only 2 to 4 patties at a time to prevent patties from touching.
5. Let the patties brown, then turn and brown the other side.
6. Remove the patties.
7. If cooking more patties, add more butter (note: the butter is necessary to keep the patties from sticking to the pan) and repeat dropping in batter and browning.
8. Serve hot.

Desserts

Old Fashioned Banana Pudding

¼ cup flour
1/8 tsp salt
¾ cup sugar
2 cups milk
3 eggs
1 tsp vanilla
4 bananas
1 box vanilla wafers

1. In a double boiler, mix flour, salt, sugar and milk.
2. Cook while stirring about 15 minutes.
3. Remove from heat and add beaten egg yolks.
4. Return to double boiler and cook 3 minutes more.
5. Remove from heat and add vanilla.
6. Layer wafers and bananas.
7. Pour pudding over wafers and bananas and repeat layers.

Meringue
3 egg whites
2 tbsp sugar

1. Beat egg whites and add sugar.
2. Beat until forms stiff peaks and put on top of pudding.
3. Brown in oven.

Chocolate Oatmeal Cookies

2 cups sugar
1 cup butter
½ cup milk
4 tbsp cocoa
2 ½ cups oatmeal
½ cup peanut butter
2 tsp vanilla

1. Mix together sugar, butter, milk and cocoa in a saucepan and boil 1 ½ minutes.
2. Remove and add the oatmeal, peanut butter and vanilla, then drop by spoonful's onto wax paper. Yields 20.

Perfect Meringue

1 tbsp cornstarch
2 tbsp cold water
½ cup boiling water
3 egg whites
6 tbsp sugar
1 tsp vanilla
Pinch of salt

1. Blend cornstarch and cold water in saucepan; add boiling water
2. Cook and stir until clear and thickened.
3. Let cool completely.
4. Beat egg whites until foamy; gradually add sugar and beat until stiff but not dry.
5. Add vanilla and salt and gradually beat in cornstarch mixture; beat well.
6. Spread meringue over cooked pie and bake at 350° for about 10 minutes. Yields   topping for two pies.
Meringue cuts beautifully and never gets sticky.

Peach Cobbler

4 cups fresh peaches, chopped, add 2 cups of water
5 breakfast biscuits, cooked and crumbled
½ cup butter, melted
1 cup sugar or ⅔ cup honey
1 egg, beaten
1 tablespoon flour
1 teaspoon almond extract

1. Cook the peaches and water in a saucepan for 6-8 minutes.
2. Pour the peaches into a 2-quart well-greased baking dish.
3. Cover with the biscuit crumbs.
4. Cream together the remaining ingredients, which makes a sticky dough.
5. Pour this dough mixture over the peaches and breadcrumbs.
6. Bake at 350°F for 30 minutes, or until brown.

Pies

Butterscotch Pie

1 cup brown sugar
¼ cup flour
1 cup cream
2 egg yolks
½ stick melted butter
1 tsp vanilla
1 cup boiling water

1. Combine sugar, flour, and cream.
2. Mix and add water, yolks, butter, and vanilla.
3. Cook over medium heat until thick while stirring.
4. Pour into 9-inch baked pie shell.

Apple Buttermilk Pie

2 medium Granny Smith apples
3 eggs
1 ½ cups sugar, divided
1 cup buttermilk
1/3 cup butter, melted
2 tbsp all-purpose flour
2 tsp ground cinnamon, divided
2 tsp vanilla
¾ tsp ground nutmeg, divided
1 9-inch unbaked pie shell
Whipped cream and additional ground cinnamon (optional)

1. Preheat oven to 350°F. Peel and core apples; cut into small chunks. Place apples in small bowl; cover with cold water and set aside.
2. Beat eggs in medium bowl with electric mixer at low speed until blended. Add all but 1 teaspoon sugar, buttermilk, butter, flour, 1 teaspoon cinnamon, vanilla and ½ teaspoon nutmeg; beat at low speed until well blended.
3. Drain apples thoroughly, place in unbaked pie shell. Pour buttermilk mixture over apples. Combine remaining 1 teaspoon sugar, 1 teaspoon cinnamon and ¼ teaspoon nutmeg in small bowl; sprinkle over top.
4. Bake 50-60 minutes or until knife inserted into center comes out clean. Serve warm or at room temperature. Garnish with whipped cream and additional cinnamon. Store leftovers in refrigerator. *Makes 8 servings*

Fresh Sour Cherry Pie

1 prepared double pie crust
4 ½ cup pitted cherries
2/3 cup white sugar
¼ cup corn starch
 1 teaspoon almond extract
1 Tablespoon unsalted butter, melted

1. Preheat oven to 400° F
2. In a bowl, stir the ingredients (except butter) together until thoroughly combined
3. Place first crust into pan and then pour filling into crust
4. Pour filling into crust
5. Place 2nd layer over cherries—cut an "X" into crust
6. Brush crust with melted butter
7. Place pie on a large baking sheet and bake 20 minutes
8. Then turn the temperature down to 375° F
9. Bake an additional 30-35 minutes
10. Remove pie from oven and allow to cool for 3 hours giving the pie filling time to thicken.

Buttermilk Pie

6 tablespoons unsalted butter
6 tablespoons all-purpose flour
1 ½ cups dark brown sugar
2 cups buttermilk
¼ teaspoon salt
3 large eggs, lightly beaten
2 teaspoons vanilla extract

1. Melt butter in medium saucepan over medium heat.
2. Remove from heat, whisk in flour until it becomes a smooth paste.
3. Add brown sugar and stir to combine, then return to heat and add in milk and salt. Cook, stirring constantly, over medium heat until mixture thickens, about 5 to 10 minutes.
4. Reduce heat and continue cooking 1 to 2 minutes more. Remove from heat.
5. Pour a small amount of the pudding into a small bowl with the beaten egg yolks and whisk vigorously to temper the egg yolks and bring them to temperature.
6. Once the egg mixture is combined and smooth, add mixture back to the original pot with the remainder of the pudding and turn the heat back onto medium high.
7. Bring to a boil as you whisk constantly for 2 more minutes.
8. Remove from heat, whisk in vanilla extract.
9. Pour pudding mix into a baked pie shell and smooth out the top.
10. Cool. Cover. Refrigerate at least 6 hours or overnight to allow the filling to set.

Fresh Strawberry Pie

1-quart fresh strawberries washed and sliced. Set aside.

Cook together until thickened, stirring constantly:
¼ cup corn starch
1 cup sugar
2/3 cup water

Remove from heat, then stir in 1 teaspoon of red food coloring and prepared strawberries. Pour into unbaked pie shell. Take top layer of pie crust, cut it into strips then lay them crisscross on top of the strawberries. Bake 400° F for 35 to 40 minutes or until brown.

Mama's Green Tomato Pie

3 cups sliced green tomatoes, drained
6 tablespoons lemon juice
1 ⅓ cups sugar
4 teaspoons grated lemon rind
3 tablespoons flour
½ teaspoon cinnamon
¼ teaspoon salt
2 tablespoons butter

1. Mix all ingredients together, but the butter.
2. Line a large pie pan with pastry.
3. Lay tomatoes, then cover with filling, then repeat a second layer.
4. Dot the top with butter.
5. Cover the pie with a top crust.
6. Bake 40 minutes at 400°F until golden brown.

Cakes

Shoofly Cupcakes

4 cups all-purpose flour
2 cups packed brown sugar
¼ tsp salt
1 cup cold butter, cubed
2 tsp baking soda
2 cups boiling water
1 cup molasses

1. Preheat oven to 350°.
2. In a large bowl, combine flour, brown sugar, and salt.
3. Cut in butter until crumbly.
4. Set aside 1 cup for topping.
5. Add baking soda to the remaining crumb mixture.
6. Stir in water and molasses.
7. Fill paper-lined muffin cups two-thirds full.
8. Sprinkle with the reserved crumb mixture.
9. Bake for 20-25 minutes or until a toothpick inserted near the center comes out clean.
10. Cool for 10 minutes before removing from pans to wire racks to cool.

Easy Fruit Cake

This recipe was one of my Daddy's favorites. For it reminded him of his childhood and the cakes his mother made for him and her family. Each year, during the summer months, his mother canned many jars of fruit preserves and applesauce. Daddy and his siblings gathered, then cracked the walnuts and pecans. Raisins were 5 cents a box, sugar was 9 cents a bag (1910-1920's), so this cake was baked every year. Delicious with a cold glass of milk or hot cup of coffee.

1 cup butter, softened
3 large eggs, room temperature
2 cups sugar
2 cups unsweetened applesauce
3 cups sifted all-purpose flour
1 cup raisins
1 cup chopped pecans
1 cup chopped black walnuts
1 cup pear or peach preserves
1 cup strawberry or cherry preserves
1 teaspoon baking soda, mixed into applesauce
1 teaspoon each: nutmeg, cinnamon, and cloves

1. Preheat the oven 250°.
2. Butter, then flour sides and bottom of pan generously. Set aside.
3. Cream butter and sugar until light and fluffy. Add eggs, one at a time, beating well after each addition.
4. Add raisins, nuts, and preserves. Then applesauce and soda. Add flour and spices and mix well.
5. Bake for 3-4 hours. Check for doneness after baking for 3 hours, as in some ovens 4 hours is too long. Cake is done when dark brown and pulls away from the sides of the pan.

Easy Fruit Cake
continued

6. Cool. Turn out. Best if made 2-3 weeks before serving to allow flavors to blend and "cure".
7. Wrap tightly in towels or todays Saran wrap. Refrigerate and keep to the day of serving.

Icebox Cake

2 cups heavy whipping cream
2 tbsp confectioners' sugar
1 tsp vanilla extract
1 9 oz. package chocolate wafers
Chocolate curls, optional

1. In a large bowl, beat cream until soft peaks form.
2. Add sugar and vanilla; beat until stiff.
3. Spread heaping teaspoonfuls on the cookies.
4. Make six stacks of cookies; turn stacks on edge and place on a serving platter, forming a 14-   in.-long cake
5. Frost top and sides with remaining whipped cream.
6. Garnish with chocolate curls if desired.
7. Refrigerate for 4-6 hours before serving.

Helpful Hint-For best whipped-cream results, think cold. Start with cold whipping cream and place the bowl and beaters in the freezer for at least 15 minutes before using.

Orange Slice Cake

2 sticks butter
2 cups sugar
4 eggs
1 cup buttermilk
1 tsp baking soda
3 ½ cups plain flour
1 lb. box chopped dates
1 lb. orange slice candy (cut up)
1 cup Angel Flake coconut (packed)
2 cups pecans (chopped)
2 tsp vanilla

TOPPING
1 cup orange juice
2 cups confectioners' sugar

1. Cream butter and sugar, add eggs one at a time, beating well after each.
2. Add flour and milk, beginning and ending with flour.
3. Roll nuts, dates and candy in flour and add to batter; add coconut.
4. Bake in a tube pan, lined with greased and floured heavy paper.
5. Use a brown bag cut to fit pan bottom.
6. Bake at 300° for 1 ½ hours or until inserted toothpick comes out dry.
7. To prepare topping: mix ingredients and pour over cake as soon as removed from oven. Let   stand overnight or until cool. Run knife around pan and remove.

Blackberry Jam Cake

1 cup butter, softened
2 cups sugar
4 eggs
2 egg yolks (Save the egg whites for frosting)
2 cups blackberry jam
3 cups all-purpose flour, divided
1 teaspoon baking powder
1 teaspoon baking soda
1 teaspoon cinnamon
1 teaspoon all-spice
1 teaspoon cloves
1 cup buttermilk
1 cup chopped pecans
2 ¾ cup raisins
Pecan halves for decoration

1. Set oven to 350° F.
2. Cream butter.
3. Gradually add sugar, beating well at medium speed.
4. Add whole eggs and egg yolks, one at a time, beating well after each addition.
5. Add jam. Beat well, then set aside.
6. In a separate bowl, combine 2 ¾ cups flour, baking powder, soda, spices.
7. Add to creamed mixture, alternating flour with buttermilk. Begin and end with the flour. Mix well after each addition.
8. Let batter sit.
9. Add remaining ¼ cup flour to a bowl with nuts and raisins. Thoroughly coat nuts and raisins.
10. Fold floured nuts and raisins into the batter. Stir well, by hand, to ensure nuts and raisins are equally distributed.

Blackberry Jam Cake
continued

11. Grease 3 round cake pan, then lightly dust the bottom with flour, Divide batter equally between the pans.
12. Bake at 350* for 40 to 45 minutes or until wooden pick comes out clean. The blackberry jam makes a dark batter. Use care to NOT overbake.
13. Cool in pans for 10 minutes.
14. Remove the cake layers from pan. Place on a wire rack. Let cool at room temperature.
15. Spread butter frosting between layers. Drizzle over top and sides of cake.
16. Garnish with nut halves. Let chill several hours. Makes one 3-layer cake.
17. Top with Butter frosting (next page).

Butter Frosting

1 cup butter (room temperature)
2 cups sugar
1 cup plain milk
2 egg whites (room temperature)

1. Combine butter, sugar, milk in large saucepan. Stir well.
2. Place over medium-high heat. Bring to boil. Stirring constantly to avoid scorching.
3. Cook until mixture reaches a soft boil stage. Test by dropping a bit of the mixture into a glass of cold water. When a soft boil forms upon heating the water and sinks to the bottom of the glass, remove mixture from the heat and cool while preparing egg whites.
4. Beat egg whites until they form stiff peaks.
5. Add about half a cup of icing mixture to egg whites. Beat to incorporate.
6. Continue to add ladles of icing mixture while beating into egg whites.
7. Beat until mixture cools slightly and thickens to a drizzling consistency (about 10 minutes).
8. Place first layer on a cake plate.
9. Put a third of the icing on this layer.
10. Add the second cake layer and cover it with 1/3 of the icing.
11. Add the top layer, gently spread remaining third of the icing over the top of the cake. Allow to drip down the sides.

Honey-Kissed Irish Whiskey Cake

4 large eggs, plus 2 yolks
¼ cup vegetable oil
1 tablespoon vanilla extract
Zest of 1 lemon, grated fine
1/3 cup honey
1 cup buttermilk, divided
2 ½ cups all-purpose flour
1 cup sugar
2 ½ teaspoons baking powder
½ teaspoon salt
1 ½ sticks unsalted butter, room temperature, cut into 1-inch chunks

Whiskey Glaze
½ cup unsalted butter
¼ cup water
½ cup sugar
½ cup honey
½ cup Irish Whiskey
Pinch of salt

1. Preheat oven to 350° F. Generously butter and flour a 12 cup Bundt pan.
2. In a small bowl, whisk together the eggs, yolks, oil, vanilla, lemon zest, honey, and ½ of the buttermilk. Set aside.
3. Sift the flour, sugar, baking powder, and salt into a mixture bowl. Mix on low speed to combine the dry ingredients.

Honey-Kissed Irish Whiskey Cake
continued

4. Toss the chunks of butter into the flour mixture and add the remaining buttermilk. Mix on medium high for 2-3 minutes. Scrape the bowl and beater. With the mixer running, add the egg mix in 3 batches, scraping the bowl between each addition.
5. Pour the batter into the prepared pan. Bake until the cake springs back when lightly pressed or a toothpick inserted in the center comes out clean, about 40 minutes.
6. While the cake bakes, make the glaze. Put the butter, water, sugar, and honey is a small saucepan. Bring the mixture to a boil, reduce to simmer and cook 5 minutes, stirring constantly. Remove the pot from heat and stir in the whiskey.
7. As soon as the cake comes out of the oven and while it's still in the pan, generously brush the cake with some of the glaze. Cool in the pan for 15 minutes. Then turn the cake out into a clean baking sheet.
8. Brush the entire top and sides of the cake with glaze, allow the glaze to absorb and repeat brushing until all the glaze is used up. Allow the cake to cool completely. Wrap in plastic wrap and set aside for 1 day to allow the flavors to develop.
9. Not recommended for children.

War Cake

1 ½ cup seedless raisins
¾ cup butter softened
¾ cup honey
3 eggs, well beaten
2 ¼ cup sifted all-purpose flour
2 ¼ teaspoon baking powder
¼ teaspoon salt
¾ teaspoon vanilla extract
¾ teaspoon lemon extract

2. Rinse raisins, drain on a paper towel, and cut fine with scissors.
3. Work butter with a spoon until fluffy and creamy, gradually add honey, while continuing to work with a spoon.
4. Work beaten eggs into batter and blend.
5. Gradually stir in sifted dry ingredients, then beat with a spoon until smooth.
6. Add extracts, raisins, and stir to blend.
7. Pour into greased and lightly floured 9x5x3 cake pan.
8. Bake in preheated oven 300°F for 2 hours or until done

Old Fashioned Molasses Cake

2 tablespoons butter, softened
¼ cup brown sugar
1 large egg, room temperature
½ cup molasses
1 cup all-purpose flour
1 teaspoon baking soda
¼ teaspoon ground ginger
¼ teaspoon ground cinnamon
1/8 teaspoon salt
½ cup hot water

1. In a small bowl, beat butter and sugar until crumbly, about 2 minutes.
2. Beat in egg.
3. Beat in molasses.
4. Combine flour, baking soda, ginger, cinnamon, and salt and sift together.
5. Add the batter and sugar mixture alternatively with the hot water, mixing well after each addition.
6. Transfer to a 9-inch square baking pan coated with cooking spray.
7. Bake 350° F for 25 to 30 minutes or until a toothpick inserted in center comes out clean.
8. Cool on a wire rack.
9. Cut into squares. If desired, covered with whipped topping.

CAUTION: Use ONLY freshly made molasses from a farmer. Store bought molasses are a different product.

Nora's German Chocolate Cake

2 (4 oz.) German's sweet chocolate baking bars, chopped
½ cup strong brewed hot coffee
2 ¼ cups all-purpose flour, divided, plus more for pan
1 teaspoon baking soda
½ teaspoon salt
1 cup butter, softened
1 cup sugar
1 cup packed light brown sugar
4 large eggs, separated
2 teaspoons vanilla extract
1 cup buttermilk

1. Preheat oven to 350° F.
2. Stir together chopped chocolate and hot coffee in medium bowl until melted and smooth, 30 seconds to one minute, stirring constantly. Set aside.
3. Whisk together flour, baking soda, and salt in a medium bowl. Beat butter and sugars until light and fluffy, about 3 minutes.
4. Add yolks, one at a time, beating just until blended after each addition.
5. Add melted chocolate mixture and vanilla and beat on low speed until blended.
6. Add flour mixture alternatively with buttermilk, beginning and ending with flour mixture. Beat until just blended after each addition.
7. Place egg whites in a separate clean bowl and beat until stiff peaks form. Gently fold into batter.
8. Divide batter among three greased (with shortening) and floured 9-inch round cake pans.

Nora's German Chocolate Cake
continued

9. Bake in preheated oven until a wooden pick inserted in center comes out clean, 24 to 28 minutes.
10. Remove pans from oven; gently run a knife around outer edge of cake layers to loosen from sides of pans.
11. Cool in pans on wire racks 15 minutes. Remove cakes from pans, transfer to wire racks.
12. Cool completely, about 1 hour.

Coconut-pecan frosting

1 (12 oz.) can evaporated milk
¾ cup butter
¾ cup sugar
¾ cup packed light brown sugar
6 egg yolks, lightly beaten
2 cups sweetened flaked coconut
2 cups chopped toasted pecans
½ teaspoon vanilla extract

1. Stir together milk, butter, sugars, and egg yolks in a heavy 3-quart saucepan. Cook over medium heat, stirring constantly, until butter melts and sugars dissolve, 3-4 minutes.
2. Cook, stirring constantly, until mixture is bubbling and reaches a pudding-like thickness, 12-14 more minutes. Remove from heat, stir in coconut, pecans, and vanilla.
4. Transfer to a bowl. Let stand, stirring occasionally, until slightly warm and spreading consistency, about 40 minutes.
4. Don't spread the frosting the usual way – it's too thick. Press it gently into the sides and top of the cake using a small spatula.
5. Cover the pie with a top crust.
6. Bake 40 minutes at 400°F until golden brown.

This & That

Honey-Made Lemonade (makes 12 cups)

9 cups water (divided)
2/3 to 1 cup honey
2 cups freshly squeezed lemon juice

1. Warm 2 cups of the water and the honey in a pot over low heat, stirring to dissolve the honey and once dissolved remove from the heat.
2. Pour the remaining 7 cups of water into the first water, stir in lemon juice.
3. Add more honey, if desired.

Acknowledgements

I especially thank my Lord Jesus Christ for my precious mother and father and my God honoring upbringing they taught me

A heartfelt "THANK YOU" to the very special people who helped make this book possible.

Deborah Culler – award winning acrylic artist for the cover painting.

Melissa Barr – typing services

Darby Culler – photo editing and editor in chief

Jessica Culler – typing service

Melissa Culler – typing service, proof reading, and helpful suggestions. Without her help, this book would never have been finished!

Darby Culler- photo editor and editor in chief

Bonnie Hatcher – proof reading, editor, and whose encouraging words kept me going until I was able to finish my family's story.

Nathan Culler-sharing jokes his grandfather, Jacob, had shared with him.

Andrea Johnson for the pictures of her father, Aubrey Mosley, and sharing some of his WWII experiences.

Donnis and Ellen Ayers for the picture of Uncle Herbert standing on his horse's saddle.

Amy Snyder-Mt. Airy Museum of Regional History-old photos and the correct spelling of the word: Asphidity.

A *special* thank you to my niece
Phyllis, and her husband, Mike Oehman, who now
own Daddy's farm and are keeping it just as green
and manicured as Daddy left it.
This book tells of my childhood growing up in the
Southwestern tip of Patrick County, Virginia.
Some of my family may have more or different
memories, but these are mine. In the early 1970s,
the house was struck by lightning and burned to
the ground, but the well still holds fresh water, the
mountains are still a velvet blue, and the spirit of
the Lord still resides over the place.

Made in the USA
Columbia, SC
01 October 2021